What Would You
Do If You
Ran the World?

Everyday Ideas from Women Who Want
to Make the World a Better Place

D1016251

Shelly Rachanow

Conari Press

First published in 2009 by Conari Press,
an imprint of Red Wheel/Weiser, LLC
With offices at:
500 Third Street, Suite 230
San Francisco, CA 94107
www.redwheelweiser.com

ISBN: 978-1-57324-358-2

Library of Congress Cataloging-in-Publication Data
available upon request.

Cover and interior design by Maija Tollefson
Typeset in Filosofia and Grotesque
Author photo by Simon Gluckman

Printed in Hong Kong
SS
10 9 8 7 6 5 4 3 2 1

*For every woman who is ready to imagine
what's possible. And to every woman
who has already showed us:*

Thank you!

Contents

What Would You Do . . . for Your Loved Ones?

What Would You Do . . . for Your Community?

What Would You Do . . . for the World?

Introduction

What would you do if you ran the world?

That's a question I've thought a lot about recently, ever since I posed it in my first book, *If Women Ran the World, Sh*t Would Get Done.* Since that book's release, so many women have shared with me ideas for making the world a better place, ideas of things we can do for ourselves, our loved ones, our community, and the world. Time after time I've thought, "If these women ran the world, just imagine what would get done!"

What Would You Do If YOU Ran the World is all about inspiring possibility . . . and turning possibility into reality. Inside you'll find a bunch of the brave, beautiful, brilliant, and totally doable ideas that women have shared with me . . . and a whole lot more. I hope you will be moved, motivated, and inspired like I have been by all the wonderful, amazing, stupendous, inspiring, and butt-kicking women out there who want to make a difference, have ideas for doing so, and are already showing the world how to get it done!

Anne Frank once said, "How wonderful it is that nobody need wait a single moment before starting to improve the world." I say we take her brave, beautiful, and brilliant advice and start today.

What are some of YOUR brave, beautiful, and brilliant ideas?

How do YOU want to make things better for yourself, your loved ones, your community, and the world?

What would you do if YOU ran the world?

What Would You Do . . . for Yourself?

Have you ever called yourself the kind of names a sailor would be embarrassed to say?

Have you ever had the kind of job that was more painful to go to than a root canal?

Have you ever had a dream, but didn't feel good enough (or young enough, pretty enough, or talented enough) for it to come true?

If you ran the world, wouldn't one of the first things you'd do for yourself be to give yourself permission to live the life YOU want to live? Wouldn't you feel powerful enough (not to mention good enough, young enough, pretty enough, and talented enough) to say *Yes* to your dreams? Wouldn't you know that you deserve to be treated with love, respect, and kindness from other people . . . and from yourself? Wouldn't you realize that, if the world trusted you to be in charge, you must be pretty darn fabulous after all?

If you ran the world, wouldn't you realize you're entitled to have some fun (and wouldn't you let yourself)? Would you hop on a plane and see all the places you've ever wanted to see? Would you find time to dance, paint, shop, write, hike, or camp? Would you let yourself take a day off every now and then?

If you ran the world, wouldn't you realize that, as Oprah Winfrey once said, "it is possible for you to do whatever you choose."

Think about it: What would you do for yourself if YOU ran the world?

10 Things You Can Do For Yourself . . . Without Ever Needing a Reason Why

1. Take a day off.

2. Easily say no when you want to . . . and feel *great* instead of *guilty* while doing so.

3. Celebrate how fabulously brilliant you are.

4. Realize that demand can be an okay thing for you to do.

5. Have regular *Pamper Yourself* time that you never, ever, *ever* consider rescheduling.

6. Take a chance.

7. Take another day off . . . this time from everything and everyone.

8. Treat yourself to something that can be described with one or more of the following adjectives: *sparkly, yummy, divine, rich, adventurous, adorable, posh, sexy, beautiful, fun,* and *exhilarating.*

9. Love, accept, and respect yourself exactly as you are (and understand that your opinion of you is the only one that counts).

10. Know that you deserve to have an infinite number of items on this list! Go ahead and add some more.

A *Doing for Myself* Story

For as long as she can remember, Karyn has been putting other people before herself. Like many teenagers who spent years feeling that Dad "just didn't understand," she left home at eighteen to ride off into the sunset with the first Prince Charming who came along. Unfortunately, Karyn's Mr. Charming turned out to be anything but that.

Karyn put her boyfriend's needs before her own for the better part of a year, even quitting her own job (at his insistence) after he lost his job and couldn't bear to be less than her in any way. Just after she'd finally gained the courage (and felt safe enough) to leave him, she found out she was pregnant. Her son, Ryan, was born six months later. Karyn was twenty years old.

Between school, a job, a new baby, and a new boyfriend (who was more like a second child than a grownup), taking time for herself was something Karyn didn't have any time to think about, let alone do. That was all the more true after she got married and gave birth to twin girls . . . and even more so after she divorced and found herself caring for three kids on her own. Most days, the best thing Karyn could do for herself and her kids was making sure they survived.

All that changed when someone asked Karyn some questions she'll never forget: "How are your kids going to view the way you treat yourself and implement that into their lives? What is your son learning about valuing women? What are your girls learning about valuing themselves?"

That's when Karyn realized she'd learned to put other people first after years of watching her mom (like so many moms) do just that. The more Karyn thought about it, the more she realized that she didn't want her kids to end up in the women-always-come-last caboose. She realized she did not want her girls to become women who *always* waited until after everyone else had eaten to eat, or walked by the shiny-happy-sparkly item on the shelf thinking, *If only that could be for me.*

Karyn decided it was time to teach her kids a new habit. She began treating herself to something she really wanted (versus needed) with every paycheck she received, even if that something was as simple as a new pair of underpants or as special as time for her favorite dance class at the gym. Even though the habit was harder to stick to than a new exercise routine at first, the words "I matter" soon became Karyn's new theme. She realized once and for all that taking time for herself is a habit that neither she nor her kids . . . nor any woman . . . should ever live without!

Wouldn't Your Life Be a Better Place If . . .

Eleanor Roosevelt once said, "No one can make you feel inferior without your consent." Take her advice and stop consenting to being overworked, used, abused, dumped on, or less than in anyway. You will have much more fun when you join with Aretha and claim the R-E-S-P-E-C-T you deserve.

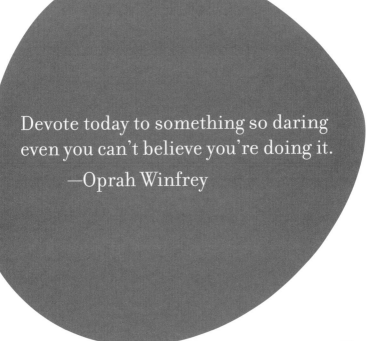

Devote today to something so daring
even you can't believe you're doing it.
—Oprah Winfrey

A *Doing for Myself* Story

Liz has always been one of those people who has done what is expected of her. Even though she had, as she says, her "mouthy and rebellious" moments, in the end she always followed the socially acceptable path. Doing the "right" thing was something she never questioned.

For Liz, doing the right thing led to many exceptional early accomplishments. She started taking courses at a local community college when she was sixteen years old, and unlike many kids her age who spent time planning for prom or homecoming, Liz was already planning (and paying) for her future (she paid for her college courses, her car, and her cell phone). She also worked several fabulous jobs that looked even more fabulous on her résumé. If there was an award for doing exactly what she "should be" doing, Liz would have won top prize.

When Liz was nineteen years old (and attending a four-year college full-time), her stepfather passed away. As Liz says, his death was an awakening for her. She realized that no matter what her stepfather had done in his life . . . be it building a house on Maryland's Eastern shore, raising birds and dogs, or skydiving . . . he felt joy and passion with everything he chose to do (otherwise he didn't do it). Liz also realized that she felt absolutely no joy or passion in any of the things she was doing . . . and she wasn't sure she ever had.

Even though Liz didn't have all the answers, and she certainly didn't know what was next for her, she knew she no longer wanted to live if she wasn't really loving what she was doing (or as she says, if she wasn't really living). She quit school and each of her jobs (all five of them) and gave herself permission to figure out what brought her joy and passion. Now, as Liz is just a few weeks away from moving across the country to start attending a new school (where she can explore organic foods and organic living, one of the deep passions she discovered), she will tell you that there are still many things that she is trying to figure out. She will also tell you that no matter how scary the unknown or new may seem, it is such a better place to be than being stuck in the place of numbness, shoulds, and regrets.

Wouldn't Your Life Be a Better Place If . . .

Marcia Wieder once said, "Fill your life with as many moments and experiences of joy and passion as you humanly can." Even if you don't exactly know what that means or looks like for you, know that you don't ever have to settle for *any* moments or experiences (or people) that do the

A Brave, Beautiful, and Brilliant Inspiration

What is right for one soul may not be right for another. It may mean having to stand on your own and do something strange in the eyes of others.

— Eileen Caddy

Have you ever wondered what might happen to a woman who was denied admission to twenty medical schools because she lacked a Y-chromosome? Have you ever wondered what might happen if this woman refused to accept that there were limits to "a woman's place"? Have you ever wondered what might happen when that woman was a trailblazer named Patsy Mink?

Patsy Mink was born in Maui in 1927, and she was never one to be shy about speaking her mind (she remembers holding onto her brother's shirt as a four-year-old and demanding . . . and winning . . . the right to accompany him to first grade). The willingness to speak up helped Patsy Mink win many things during her early life, including the election for student body president at her high school and a battle against segregated student housing at the University of Nebraska. And when medical school after medical school said *No* to Patsy Mink, there was no way she was going to let them have the last word. Deciding that the best way she could make all schools accept women was to become a lawyer, Patsy Mink said *Yes* to the University of Chicago Law School, graduating in 1951 and becoming the first woman of Japanese American ancestry to practice law in Hawaii.

When both her race and her gender made it difficult for Patsy Mink not only to find her first job but also to find acceptance from many of her male counterparts, she decided to speak up and speak out on an even greater scale. Patsy Mink was first elected to Hawaii's Territorial House in 1956 and then to the Territorial Senate in 1958. In 1964, she became the first Asian American woman to serve in Congress, doing so from 1964 to 1977 and again from 1990 until her death in 2002. In every political place Patsy Mink served, she spoke up and spoke out so that all women could experience the respect and fair treatment she'd been denied.

Of all the amazing things Patsy Mink did for herself and for women, one of the greatest was her drafting of Title IX, which was enacted on June 23, 1972, and which mandated equal support for males and females in academics and athletics at any institution receiving federal money. Because of Title IX, schools can no longer prevent women from wielding a scalpel or shouting "Fore!" just because of our XX genes. With Title IX, Patsy Mink proved to the world (and to herself) just how powerful women are when we speak up and speak out about the things we care about the most.

Is there some way YOU want to speak up, speak out, and "stand on your own"?

An Awesome Idea in Action

Have you ever paid a plumber a huge sum of money for a job that only took him five minutes to finish?

Have you ever asked someone from the Y-chromosome set to fix something for you and then waited forever for him to get it done?

Have you ever found yourself living alone and utterly terrified of the words *leak, drip, break, rot,* or *flood*?

If you can answer *Yes* to any of those questions (or, if you're like me, *Yes* to all three), then you can join me in breathing a huge, collective, empowering sigh of relief. Now we don't need to be broke, frustrated, or terrified. We just need to Be Jane!

Be Jane is an online community that was started in 2003 by Heidi Baker and Eden Jarrin. It was inspired by Heidi's own experience in purchasing her first home, which had, as she says, "yellowed popcorn ceilings, carpet that made a game of 'Guess That Stain,' and a fireplace that looked like it belonged on *That '70s Show.*" Stunned by the price quotes she received from repair*men,* Heidi Baker decided she was not going to let anyone rip her off. She ignored all the naysayers and head shakers at the home improvement store and fixed up her home herself, eventually selling it for more than twice what she paid for it! In the process, she also realized that her XX genes (like yours and mine) are capable of more than she had ever dreamed.

Heidi Baker and Eden Jarrin created Be Jane so that women everywhere "could learn through home improvement to gain confidence in their abilities to truly make a difference in the way they live." The site contains a growing list of articles, tips, tutorials, and how to's, as well as plenty of inspiration for midproject, when the dirt and dust have gotten a bit too much to bear. I particularly love the JQ, or Jane Quotient, that rates projects from one hammer to five hammers based on ease or difficulty (I'm hoping to brave some two hammer projects soon). I also love the featured Janes, other everyday women who aren't afraid to share their own thoughts, triumphs, and what-have-I-done moments.

These days, more and more women are becoming home owners on their own, and thanks to Be Jane, we can learn to navigate the aisles of any home improvement store just as easily as we can the levels of a department store. Thanks to Be Jane, we don't ever have to fear those scary sounds that used to cause us to run screaming for the Yellow Pages. Because when it comes down to it, no one should ever stand in the way of a woman who has decided she is going to get something done. This is especially true when that woman is holding a power tool!

Here's an Idea You Can Do for Yourself *Today* . . .
Check out *www.BeJane.com* and learn more about creating a space YOU will love!

A *Doing for Myself* Story

As a child, my sister Mindy was the tomboy of our family. She was always outside playing football, soccer, baseball, and every sport imaginable with the boys in the neighborhood, ready to prove she could beat all of them (and she usually could). Feeling great and being in great shape were never things she had to worry about.

Time for sports dwindled when Mindy started college and papers, internships, and a heavy class load seemed to eat up all the spare hours in her day. This was all the more true the summer after she graduated when she took her Occupational Therapist Certification Exam and was married all in a matter of months. When Mindy returned from her honeymoon, she started working full-time. Not only did she have even less time to exercise than when she was in college, her job entailed visiting clients in schools and homes around Baltimore. Eating healthy was a challenge, especially in the days when it seemed like the only quick choices were "super-sized."

As is the case for most women, Mindy's time became even more limited after she became a mom. Even though she reduced her weekly workload from forty hours to thirty-two hours, Mindy experienced intense periods of fatigue that can only be described as PMS gone wild. When the sensation lasted longer than the normal post-pregnancy experience, she decided to have a round of tests and blood work done. While Mindy breathed easier when each test came back normal, part of her knew that something wasn't quite right with her body. She also knew she needed to figure out what that was.

Mindy's answer came when she decided to see an endocrinologist who determined she was pre-diabetic (on a scale of 0 to 10, with 10 being diabetic, Mindy was at a 9). Mindy's doctor told her that if she didn't start exercising and eating better immediately, she would no longer be able to enjoy the chocolate-peanut butter soy shakes she loves so much, or play with her active and athletic son the way she wanted to. While the thought of losing dessert was heartbreaking, the thought of not being able to enjoy time with her son was more tragic than any Greek play ever could be. Mindy knew it was time to take action.

For Mindy, the answer came by joining Curves. Exercising for thirty minutes three times a week was something she felt she could handle time- and energy-wise (and the fact that there's a club two minutes from her house helped, too). Mindy also started eating a lot less bread and pasta (which for her was a worthy trade-off, since doing so meant she could still enjoy those soy shakes). In the nearly two years since Mindy took charge of her health, she has not only lost weight, she has gained great friends and great support from the other women at the club. She has also received a completely clean bill of health from her doctor. Of all the things Mindy has ever wanted to beat, this has been her sweetest victory of all.

Wouldn't Your Life Be a Better Place If . . .

As Mary Pickford said, "You may have a fresh start any moment you choose." If you're not feeling your best, make today the day you start fresh. Remember: You don't need to live up to anyone's standard for *looking* good, be it your partner's or society's. You only need to *feel* good about you. Be willing to do what you need to do so you feel your best today.

An Awesome Idea in Action

Did you know that . . .

According to the "Women and Cardiovascular Disease" section of the American Heart Association web site (*www.american-heart.org*)

❊   Only 13 percent of women view heart disease as a health threat, even though it's women's number one killer?

❊   Cardiovascular disease (CVD) kills nearly 500,000 women a year, more than the next six causes of death combined?

❊   1 in 26 female deaths are from CVD, compared with 1 in 30 from breast cancer?

In February 2004, administrators at the American Heart Association decided to do something about these statistics. They created Go Red for Women (*www.goredforwomen.org*) to celebrate the "energy, passion, and power we have as women to band together and wipe out heart disease." The Web site contains tips for how to love your heart, recipes and heart-healthy grocery lists, and important healthy heart numbers to know, like the ranges for cholesterol, body mass index, and blood pressure. There is also a list of ways you can go red to help your heart and a section with personal stories of women who have faced heart disease and made the choice to do something for their health and themselves.

As Mindy learned, no matter how fabulous your doctor is, YOU are the best advocate for your health and your body. Make the choice to love your heart today. Take advice from Go Red for Women and go red in the way that works best for you, be it by eating an apple, participating in National Wear Red Day (which occurs annually in February), or wearing a fabulous red dress (and maybe even buying it from a store that supports the cause). Trust your instincts like my sister Mindy did, and do what you need to do so you can live with the best energy, zest, and heart possible!

Here's an Idea You Can Do for Yourself *Today* . . . Check out *www.goredforwomen.org* to learn more about your heart and your health.

A *Doing for Myself* Story

Have you ever done something that your family, friends, and all those acquaintances who are fond of their own opinions disagreed with?

Have you ever made one of those grab-the-helmet-and-brace-for-impact choices that you knew was going to result in the words *crazy, stupid, immature, lazy,* or *selfish* being hurled toward you by those people who are supposed to love you the most?

Have you ever been sure something was right (or wrong) for you, even though every other person you knew, not to mention all reason and logic, seemed to say otherwise?

Not too long ago, I had to make one of those nail-biting, gray-hair-inducing, I-wonder-who's-going-to-call-me-crazy-first decisions. I received a job offer for a big bucks, big benefits, and big bonus full-time position at the temp job I'd begun several months earlier. The problem: the job was also a big *bore*!

What came next was a plethora of opinions and advice (some asked for, some not) from people who were sure *they* knew what was best for me:

❊ "You must be so relieved, the way the economy is going."

❊ "Well if you say no, what else are you going to do?"

❇ "You'd be a fool to pass this up."

❇ "Grow up already and accept the position. The time for fantasy land is long over!" (This person is now banned from my speed dial.)

❇ "Just take the job. You don't have to do it forever."

❇ "Have I mentioned you'd be a fool to pass this up?"

❇ "Why don't you work there for a year so you can save money? What's so bad about that?"

❇ "With over 1,000 employees at this company, you're sure to meet lots of cute, single guys. It could be like joining a dating service for free." (Thanks, Mom.)

❇ *"You do realize you would be a fool to pass this up?"*

As I sat among a pile of pro and con lists (and cartons of Ben & Jerry's) trying to make a decision, I realized I knew something that no one else did.

I did not want this job. I would not even remotely enjoy it.

Why would I ever let anyone convince me to do something that I knew ahead of time I would dislike? Wasn't it okay for me to trust my own opinion?

In that moment, I decided trusting myself is more than okay: it's a stop-the-presses, front-page-headline, nothing-else-is-more-noteworthy necessity!

Are you ready to change, do, leave, or join something but haven't yet because of all the reasons other people have used to convince you otherwise? Are you ready to quiet all the well-intentioned, often related to you, always certain, but ultimately clueless folks who think they know what's best for you? Are you ready to say *Yes* to something *today* that you know is right for you?

If you ran the world, wouldn't listening to your needs be as easy as meeting everyone else's needs is now? Wouldn't one of the things you do for yourself be trusting your own opinion . . . and recognizing how brilliant it really is! The next time one of your choices causes any head shaking, finger wagging, and not-so-friendly adjectives to be hurled your way, ignore them and continue on. No matter what anyone else thinks, when it comes to what's best for you, you will *always* have the smartest opinion around!

By the way, I said *No* to the job and *Yes* to my instincts. Doing so was yummier than Ben & Jerry's. It is also something I have never regretted.

Wouldn't Your Life Be a Better Place If . . .

Take some advice from Barbara Streisand: "You have to trust yourself, be what you are, and do what you ought to do the way you should do it. You have got to discover you, what you do, and trust it." And while you're at it, take the "My Opinion Rocks" pledge and honor your brilliant self today and everyday!

The *My Opinion Rocks* Pledge
From this moment forward . . .

✻ I will refuse to let any well-intentioned, often related to me, always certain, but ultimately clueless folks convince me they know what is best for me!

✻ I will ignore (and possibly remove from my speed dial) anyone who calls me or my choices crazy, stupid, immature, lazy, selfish, or anything else that's just plain mean!

✻ I will never again let anyone convince me to do something that I know ahead of time I will dislike!

✻ I will remember that when it comes to what's best for me, I will always have the smartest opinion around!

My Opinion Rocks! And so do I!

Name _____   Date _____

A *Doing for Myself* Story

Like many children growing up in Denmark, Marlene experienced the cornerstone of Scandinavian culture from an early age, the unspoken code of social conduct *Janteloven* or "Jante Law," ten rules that were created by author Aksel Sandemose and can be summed up by the phrase: *Don't think you're anyone special or that you're better than us.* The translation: Standing up for your beliefs . . . or for yourself . . . was not something she (or anyone) was ever supposed to do.

One belief Marlene has always had is that *all* people deserve equality no matter their gender, preferences, or race. That belief has only grown stronger as she moved to Germany, Norway, and then the United States for new opportunities. In each country (in schools and otherwise), Marlene noticed there were minorities who were put down and discriminated against, there were people who were made to feel like they did not fit in, there were groups less accepted than everyone else (something she has personally experienced as a gay woman). The only difference, Marlene noticed, was that each country had different definitions of what (or who) should be part of the "in crowd."

When Marlene fell in love and had to learn more about immigration law than even most lawyers care to know, she realized she had to make a choice. She realized she could continue to be a silent partner regarding the unfair treatment she's experienced, or she could speak up for herself (and maybe inspire others to do the same in the process). She could become a trendsetter on the most important red carpet of all, the one leading to her own courage. Not long ago, she took those first steps by getting involved with the Human Rights Campaign (*www.hrc.org*), a grassroots organization that promotes fairness and equal rights.

The more Marlene thought about it, she realized that standing up for herself has nothing to do with feeling better than or special. Instead, it's about saying that the right to life, liberty, and the pursuit of happiness shouldn't just apply to certain definitions of happiness. It's about saying that who we want to love and live with forever should not limit the rights we're entitled to experience. It's about realizing that each of us is worthy of an equal chance to live the life we choose to live without being judged, juried, hated, maligned, or denied the opportunity to do so. It's about realizing, "I deserve to be treated fairly *without having to change who I am.*"

Because when it comes down to it, accepting ourselves exactly as we are is one of the best things we can ever do for ourselves. Having the courage to speak out when the world disagrees is another.

Wouldn't Your Life Be a Better Place If . . .

Goldie Hawn once said, "I've finally stopped running away from myself. Who else is there better to be?" Why don't you make today the day you take her advice? After all, don't you do enough running around as it is?

An Awesome Idea in Action

Did you know that . . .

According to statistics listed on the National Domestic Violence Hotline Web site (*www.ndvh.org*),

❋ One out of three women around the world has been beaten, coerced into sex, or otherwise abused during her lifetime?

❋ One in three teens report knowing a friend or peer who has been hit, punched, slapped, choked, or physically hurt by his or her partner?

❋ Ninety-two percent of women say that reducing domestic violence and sexual assault should be at the top of any formal efforts taken on behalf of women today?

The sad truth is that for most of us, these numbers are not surprising. In my own life, among my close girlfriends, I know three women who have been abused physically or sexually either as a child or as an adult. That number grows much higher when I count acquaintances or colleagues who speak openly about their lives. I am sad to think that the same is likely true for you.

If you are currently in a relationship or situation in which you are being abused, take the advice of the National

Domestic Violence Hotline and "break the silence, make the call." The National Domestic Violence Hotline answers more than 19,000 calls each month, and they provide crisis intervention, safety planning, and a link to resources in a caller's immediate area. In addition, the Hotline's Web site has a wonderful safety planning section that includes tips for getting ready to leave, how to leave, and what to do after you leave an abusive situation. There is also a printable personal safety plan that people can download.

As the National Domestic Violence Hotline Web site says, "Violence is never right." Each of us deserves to feel truly safe, respected, and loved . . . without pain. None of us has ever done anything (or not done anything) to deserve abuse of any kind. Anyone who tells us otherwise—be it a parent, partner, counselor, boss, advisor, or religious official— is just plain wrong!

Isn't it time to stop listening to the people who don't value you? Isn't it time to stop allowing them to be right? Even if you're not currently running the world, you can run your world so it becomes a world where you feel safe. You can choose to start today, and when you are ready, know that you don't have to do it all alone.

Here's an Idea You Can Do for Yourself *Today* . . .
Check out *www.ndvh.org* or call 1-800-799-SAFE
(7233) or 1-800-787-3224 (TTY) if you need help
leaving an abusive situation or if you want to learn
more about how you can help women in need.

A *Doing for Myself* Story

When Adrienne was four years old, her mom went back to work, and like many toddlers did in the days before day care was common, Adrienne spent a lot of time at a relative's house. Unfortunately, she soon experienced something else that far too many children experience: abuse by someone she should have been able to trust.

Adrienne kept her secret for years, believing as most children in her situation do that what happened had to be her fault. *She* felt like the one who was wrong or bad. *She* felt like the one to blame. This sense of blame led to shame, and shame led to silence for a long time . . . but not forever.

As time went on, Adrienne realized that she wanted to acknowledge that she had been abused. She wanted to stop worrying about bringing other people down or making other people feel bad. *She* wanted to stop feeling bad about something that was not her fault . . . in fact, she wanted to stop being the only person who knew about her experience at all. Adrienne was ready to be hugged and held by arms that loved and supported her. She was ready to stop feeling like a victim and start defining herself by a new "V" word. She was ready to value herself.

When Adrienne did finally tell her parents what happened, she was met with more screaming and shouting than hugs and kisses. But even though her family was not ready to accept or admit that Adrienne had been abused (and to some extent still aren't, all these years later), Adrienne was ready to do so for herself. She decided she would not let her family's reaction keep her from leaving the land of blame, shame, and silence. She would not let other people stop her from reclaiming her sense of self-worth or from trusting her own authority and feelings. She would not wait for anyone else's validation to stop feeling like a victim.

For Adrienne, realizing she has the power to empower herself changed everything for her. She realized she could trust herself, her thoughts, and her feelings about every situation. She realized she is the brave, beautiful, and brilliant woman her friends have always known she is. She realized she has the power to love herself no matter what, and that is the most powerful gift of all.

Wouldn't Your Life Be a Better Place If . . .

As Oprah Winfrey once said, "It doesn't matter who you are or where you came from. The ability to triumph begins with you. *Always*." It also doesn't matter what you have experienced. No matter what has happened in your life, you can choose today to begin feeling triumphant. You can choose today to begin feeling victorious, rather than victimized.

What Do YOU Want to Do for Yourself?

Lucille Ball once said, "It's a helluva start, being able to recognize what makes you happy." It's also a helluva start letting yourself be happy. What are YOU ready to start (or stop) letting yourself do?

Are you ready to start taking more time for yourself like Karyn, taking charge of your health like Mindy, trusting your own opinion like me, or standing up for your rights like Marlene? Are you ready to stop living without joy and passion like Liz, or feeling bad about yourself like Adrienne?

Are you ready to make a fresh start when the situation requires? Are you ready to ask for help when you need it (or when help would be nice to have)? Are you ready to leave a relationship where you are undervalued and unappreciated (or are being abused)? Are you ready to ask for a promotion or to try something new (no matter how crazy or scary)? Are you ready to pursue your passion even if the well-intentioned but ultimately clueless set gives you plenty of reasons why you should do otherwise?

When it comes down to it, are you ready to live the kind of life YOU want to live?

If you ran the world, wouldn't you do what you needed to do for yourself so you could live your dream life? Wouldn't you insist that part of your royal duties included spending time doing the things you love? Certainly you would know . . . really know . . . that YOU matter. You would value yourself and know that you deserve to be valued by those around you (and not just because you may utter the phrase "off with his head"). You would love, accept, and respect yourself . . . all of yourself . . . even the parts you would never want caught on tape.

While most of us would agree that everything looks better with great accessories, the truth is we do not need a fun scepter or shiny crown on our head to live our lives that way. Today, right now, YOU can do as Golda Meir said and "create the kind of self that you will be happy to live with all your life."

Think of it this way: Before we can ever make *the* world a better place, we have to be willing to make *our* world the best world possible. Each of us deserves to receive this gift of permission from ourselves. Are YOU ready to give it?

The Brave, Beautiful, and Brilliant Things I Want to Do for Myself

_____

_____

_____

_____

_____

_____

_____

_____

_____

_____

What Would You Do . . . for Your Loved Ones?

Have you ever yawned through a whole day of work after staying up all night worrying about a child who was sick, sad, or pierced in places you never thought possible?

Have you ever held a friend's hand when she heard news from a doctor that no one should ever have to hear?

Have you ever resisted saying something mean to your spouse that would have felt so good in the moment, but so awful later?

Most of us can answer *Yes* to these questions. In fact, some of us can answer *Yes* to these questions on a weekly, daily, and hourly basis! Because when it comes to the people we love most in this world, most of us really do want them to be happy, healthy, and living their dreams . . . even if their dreams contain clothing, ideas, or partners that are different from those we would have chosen for them.

If you ran the world, wouldn't you do everything in your power to love and support the people who love and support you . . . kind of like you do now? Wouldn't you take advantage of every world-running resource available so that a great life was more than just a nice *What if* for your loved ones?

Rose Kennedy once said, "Life isn't a matter of milestones, but of moments." What kind of moments would you create with the people you care about? What kind of moments would you include in your *perfect day* day planner? What kind of moments would you cherish and treasure forever? What would you do for your loved ones if YOU ran the world?

10 Things You Can Do for Your Loved Ones . . . Often in Sixty Seconds or Less

1. Listen . . . without thinking, speaking, sighing, or rolling your eyes.

2. Make them laugh when they need to the most.

3. Bring them tissues . . . and cry with them.

4. Bring them ice cream.

5. Give them a hug.

6. Tell them they are talented, wonderful, fabulous, beautiful, brilliant, and sexy when they feel otherwise.

7. Choose to *not* tell them when you know they are wrong and you are right.

8. Accept their choices . . . without arguing, fuming, criticizing, or leaving the room.

9. Leave the room if it's the only way you can avoid arguing, fuming, or criticizing.

10. Forgive them . . . even if they never say, "I'm sorry."

A *Doing for My Loved Ones* Story

Jenn and Emily met in 1993 when Jenn was a sophomore and Emily was a freshman at Oglethorpe University in suburban Atlanta. They socialized with mutual friends for awhile, but became the best of friends when Emily rushed Jenn's sorority and Jenn was her "Owl Pal" for a week. Emily joked that Jenn probably wouldn't come back and visit her after Jenn was no longer obligated to do so. Jenn proved her wrong by knocking on Emily's door so that they could study (or not study) together every day.

Through the years, Jenn and Emily have shared many a bottle of wine as they commiserated over men, jobs, family, bad hair cuts, and most everything else friends laugh and cry about. That was especially true a few years ago, when Jenn decided to move to New Jersey and Emily to Miami. When Emily offered Jenn a pair of R.E.M. tickets just days before she was headed South and was literally knee deep in boxes, Jenn showed up at Emily's apartment with moving supplies instead. As much as Jenn loves Michael Stipe, seeing him live on stage wasn't more important than being there for her friend.

In fact, as Jenn saw it, her "friend" job description did not end once Emily's packing was complete. As everyone who knows Emily knows, she is an amazing athlete, but driving is not her sport. To make sure Emily and her car arrived in Miami in one piece, Jenn drove all but an hour and a half of the ten-hour drive. Jenn also stayed quiet when they arrived at 2:00 a.m. only to discover that Emily couldn't remember how to get to her new condo (and it took an extra hour of circling pink flamingos in South Beach until they found it).

That morning, Jenn knew it was more important for her to help her friend destress than it was to add to the stress Emily was already feeling. That's because for Jenn and Emily, and for best friends everywhere, being there is always more important than being right.

Wouldn't Your Loved Ones' Lives Be Better Places If . . .

Perhaps George Eliot said it best when she said, "What do we live for, if it is not to make life less difficult for each other?" One of the best things we can ever do for our loved ones is support them without the need to criticize, complain, compare, or lay blame . . . especially when we're wondering if strangling has a sentence of fifteen to life. Whenever possible, be there for the people you love. Doing so is always doing right.

An Awesome Idea in Action

Have you ever moved to a new area and wished you had a friend who loves eating pancakes for dinner as much as you?

Have you ever been in the middle of a meltdown and were so grateful to have someone nearby who's always willing to rush out and buy you the emergency-size bag of peanut M&Ms (and then share them with you)?

Have you ever been so darn glad that the phrase "best friends forever" isn't just something that applies to our childhood?

Then *GirlfriendsCafe.com* is a place you will love!

GirlfriendsCafe.com is a Web site where women of all ages and backgrounds can "meet" and do what girlfriends do best: chat, listen, share, and help each other remember how fabulous we are. The Web site was created by Linda and Lee, two women who have been friends for more than twenty years and who first met because they both needed to track down the same man (which, as they say, is "another story and another Web site"). That chance encounter they had while living across town from each other (and not sharing a single friend between them) was the beginning of a great friendship.

Through the years, Linda and Lee have been there as each single-handedly raised a son, had her fair share of bad dates (and bad hair colors), and needed the kind of love only a best friend and a big piece of chocolate can bring. Whether they were living in the same zip code or clear across the country, they are, as all great friends are, "always there for each other, no questions asked." As they say, and as all girlfriends know, "That's what girlfriends are for." *GirlfriendsCafe.com* is Linda and Lee's gift to women everywhere who appreciate all the amazing things true friendship brings.

Here's an Idea You Can Do for Your Loved Ones *Today* . . .
Grab some friends and check out *www.GirlfriendsCafe.com* Enjoy that all-important girl time with the women who already matter most to you, and with all the new women you can meet.

Have you ever been so glad to see a friend's phone number on your caller ID . . . only to be devastated by the news she called to share?

Have you ever heard the words *cancer, stage,* and *four* used together in a sentence about one of your best friends . . . and you lived 3,000 miles away and were unable to give her a hug?

Have you ever been so frustrated that the ability to instantly beam somewhere à la *Star Trek* doesn't already exist?

I'll never forget that February day when I answered the phone to hear my friend Peggy sound worse than she sounded when she had morning sickness every day for nine months straight. One of our best friends, Elisabeth, had just had surgery, and the doctors found something no one had expected: Cancer had broken through the wall of her colon and had spread. True, Elisabeth had been feeling tired for a while, but with a show opening at her theater, an extra-busy holiday season filled with overseas travel, and a relationship on the mend, we thought all those nap days were just from normal life stuff.

Not a day goes by that I wish ticket sales and too many trips to Harrod's had been to blame!

For Elisabeth, the past year and a half has been a revolving door of surgery, chemotherapy, depression, more surgery, more chemotherapy, hope, a disappointing second diagnosis, the decision not to have anymore chemotherapy, and time out of the country for alternative treatment. As she describes it, she feels like she has been sprinting on a treadmill: constantly moving but unable to move *forward* with everyone else.

As I am writing this story, Elisabeth has just returned to the United States, and we are volleying dates back and forth for my next visit and all the eating, shopping, and talking for days that have become our specialty. What I have learned more than anything during these past months is that no matter how full our calendars are, no deadline, conference, work schedule, or commitment is more important than time with the people we love the most.

Even if you haven't received the kind of phone call I did, the gift of time is one you can share with your family and friends every day. When you do so with readiness, willingness, and the ability to not grumble if they are late or get you horribly lost, you give your loved ones (and yourself) one of the best gifts possible.

Wouldn't Your Loved Ones' Lives Be Better Places If . . .

Maya Angelou once said, "If you ever find it in your heart to care for somebody else, you will have succeeded." Go ahead and surprise somebody YOU care about today. Play hooky and plan a fun day with them or, if you are far away, pick up the phone and call. Remember: When you enjoy the people you love every day, you succeed in the most important way possible.

An Awesome Idea in Action

If you have ever learned that a good friend has a serious illness, like my experience with Elisabeth, you know that waiting for news can be nail biting to the point where no manicure can help. And if you have ever received a diagnosis like Elisabeth's, or were the caretaker for someone who did, you know how exhausting it can be to open your eyes in the morning, much less answer a phone.

That's where *www.CarePages.com* can help.

Care Pages was started by Eric and Sharon Langshur after their son, Matthew, was diagnosed with a heart defect. The Langshurs constructed a Web site with news, pictures, and a message board so that their loved ones could stay updated with the news about Matthew. The Web site was so helpful that the Langshurs decided to start a company so that anyone who needed a Care Page could build one.

Care Pages are quick and easy to set up, and there is never a charge to create one. The Web site features articles, recipes, and inspirational stories for visitors and members alike. There are specific sections for moms and dads, and blogs with advice for both caregivers and the people being cared for. You can email a "CareCompliment" to a hospital staff member as a way to thank someone who has made a difference (and to let the hospital know how wonderful that person is). You can also send a personalized "Tell a Friend" email if you know someone who could be helped by having a Care Page.

Over the past five years, Care Pages has helped more than a million families and friends stay connected when they needed to the most. Creating a Care Page is a great way to make a hard time easier.

Here's an Idea You Can Do for Your Loved Ones *Today*. . .
Check out *www.CarePages.com* to learn more about staying connected during important and difficult times.

A *Doing for My Loved Ones* Story

Rebecca was born and raised in Georgia, and between family time, church on Sunday, and a few added pounds from her mother's homemade pot roast and cranberry delight, her childhood was pretty typical for a southern girl . . . in most ways. As the middle daughter in a family of three girls, with just five years separating them, Rebecca quickly became her family's master of sass. She also spent years shining on stages around Atlanta from the time she was six, and she particularly enjoyed playing characters who weren't the model of politeness.

Like many people who have been bitten by the acting bug, in her early twenties Rebecca left the land of fried food and sweet tea to head for Hollywood. Through her years of performing in Atlanta, she'd realized that stand-up comedy was her first love, and she began heckling audiences around Los Angeles, much to their delight. Soon she met Bobby, and three weeks after meeting him she knew she had fallen in love (of course, she didn't tell him quite so soon).

Rebecca and Bobby were soon inseparable, spending every spare minute together, be it at concerts, the beach, or Big Bear Mountain. Even with all the time they spent in the sun, they never expected to rush a dizzy and dehydrated Rebecca to the emergency room one day two years into their relationship. They were even more shocked to learn that Rebecca was pregnant (luckily, she was seated, and

Bobby, whose knees buckled, was standing in front of a chair when they heard the news).

As Rebecca says, having to call her traditional southern parents and tell them that she was pregnant was "the worst day of her life." Even as a twenty-five-year-old, the last thing she ever wanted to do was disappoint them. At Bobby's insistence, she didn't wait, and she called them that day. Despite Rebecca's quaking knees and shaking hands, her parents couldn't have been more understanding. While they shed a few tears, they didn't scream, shout, hang up, or utter the word *disown.* Instead, they expressed their love and acceptance, and offered to throw Rebecca and Bobby a wedding if they wanted one, which they did. Three months later, Rebecca and Bobby were married.

As Rebecca and Bobby approach their fifth anniversary and are now the proud parents of two beautiful boys, they know that they received more than the gift of a wedding that day from Rebecca's parents. They learned that accepting another person's choices, even and especially when those choices are different than our own, is one of the most giving acts around.

Wouldn't Your Loved Ones' Lives Be Better Places If . . .

Take some advice from Maya Angelou:
"The ache for home lives in all of us, the safe place where we can go as we are and not be questioned." For anyone who was ever picked last at recess or left out of homecoming fun, you know how horrible it feels to not be accepted. Make it a point to be the safe place for your loved ones, even when you're not quite sure it's safe for them to be around you! They will appreciate it, and you, maybe more than you will ever know.

The *I Accept Your Choices* Promise

Dear, _____

From now on, I will do my best to accept your choices even when I disagree with you, don't understand your reasons, or am convinced you've been abducted by aliens. I want you to know that as much as I love my opinion, I love you more (even when it doesn't seem like it). If your choices truly make you happy, you have my sometimes grumbling but ultimately whole-hearted support.

Love,

☀ Disclaimer: The *I Accept Your Choices* promise may need to be made more than once, and in some instances, such as those involving teenagers and husbands, more than once a minute. Use this promise as often as needed to avoid developing laryngitis or acting in ways that judges and police officers generally disapprove of.

A *Doing for My Loved Ones* Story

As a little girl, Jan was fortunate to have something many children wish for: a father who was always there for her. Throughout the years, Jan's father was always ready to lend an ear whenever she needed someone to lean on, cry to, and listen to her joy, despair, and everything in between . . . even when his hearing began to fail after decades of drilling teeth.

Jan's father was diagnosed with Alzheimer's disease in 1997, though he was fairly sure he had it long before his family or doctors ever suspected. Despite entering the University of California at San Diego's Alzheimer's research department and receiving risky experimental brain surgery in 2002, little by little, the father who had always been there for Jan began to slip away. As the disease progressed, communication became especially difficult. Jan's mom in particular had a hard time understanding what was happening. She thought if she just kept raising her voice, eventually her husband would hear her and understand. As anyone who has ever seen a loved one struggle with Alzheimer's knows, volume is not the problem or the solution.

Jan added thousands of miles to her car as she traveled the two hours from her house to her parents'. At times she acted as housekeeper, chef, pharmacist organizing med-ications, and social director, planning many a needed "girl's night out" for her mom (theater and dinner were particular favorites). She also decided to do for her dad what he had done for her for so long: she sat beside him and listened.

Using a dry erase board to communicate her questions, Jan learned about his politics, his sometimes changing religious views, his desire to go to heaven, his hatred of evil, his feelings of failure as a father and husband, his love of his family, and his fears: things his private, reserved demeanor had never let him share before. He even felt safe enough to tell her about his hallucinations, and how even though he recognized them for what they were, they were still very real to him. Jan and her dad emptied many boxes of tissues during their time together, both from laughter and from tears. They grew even closer than they had been before.

Jan's dad passed away recently, and as she thinks back over the past few years, she says, "I would never wish this disease on anyone. I wish my dad never had to suffer with it, nor we, but I also wouldn't trade the special, close times I had with my dad for anything in the world. I miss him so much, but interestingly enough, what I miss most is the closeness we developed during the past two years." As Jan and her dad learned, listening to someone is one of the best ways in the world we can love them.

Wouldn't Your Loved Ones' Lives Be Better Places If . . .

Rebecca Falls once said, "One of the most valuable things we can do to heal one another is listen to each other's stories." Think of it this way: If people have chosen to confide in you, they already know how brilliant you are. You don't need to prove it by advising, fixing, or thinking of a great response. Instead, just listen. Not only is that the smartest thing you can do, it is also the most compassionate.

A Brave, Beautiful, and Brilliant Possibility

I don't know about you, but I can't think of a single person who hasn't had to watch someone they love suffer with a debilitating illness, be it cancer like Elisabeth, Alzheimer's disease like Jan's dad, or one of the many others that can befall us. As fast and furiously as our researchers and scientists are working on finding cures for disease, I wonder if I will be here when words like *cancer* and *Alzheimer's* are relegated to their proper place in history (or *her*story) books.

Here's an idea that could help speed up the process. When a commercial comes on television, most of us go to the bathroom, grab the Ben & Jerry's, or press fast-forward on the TiVo. Wouldn't it be amazing if someone running a company made the choice to spend a fraction of their marketing budget by creating just one advertisement that said something like:

> We are so grateful to everyone who has ever tried our products and become our loyal customers. And if you have never tried our products, we sure hope you will soon . . . and we also hope you'll think they're as fabulous as we do. Ultimately, we know you'll buy our products if they work for you and you like them, so this is the only advertisement you will see about them from us from now on. Instead of spending loads of money to

repeatedly tell you that we should be your first choice, we are going to spend our advertising money in a way that will actually make a difference in this world. From now on, we are going to donate that money to the scientists and researchers who are working to cure our worst diseases and make our world a healthier place. This is not a ploy or a temporary gimmick. It is instead, quite simply, the right thing to do.

Imagine if one company made this choice. What about five companies, or ten, or one hundred? What if political candidates followed suit? I don't know about you, but hearing an advertisement like this would make me more loyal to a company, and to a candidate, than hearing a slogan ever would.

Wouldn't it be amazing if this one change in approach paved the way for millions of people to be alive and be here to enjoy their favorite must-see-TV? Think about it: we live in a world where men have walked on the moon, sheep have been cloned, and our tiniest premature babies have lived. Truly anything is possible. The only question is: Is anyone willing to take the first step?

What brave, beautiful, and brilliant possibilities can YOU suggest?

A *Doing for My Loved Ones* Story

Erica and her mom, Janet, always had a great relationship, perhaps in part because in many ways they were complete opposites. Erica is loud, boisterous, and always ready to bask in the limelight, while Janet was quiet, reserved, and more comfortable giving a hand than receiving one. For all their differences, Janet was glad to see they shared something important in common: the willingness to stand up for themselves and what mattered most to them, even if that meant rebelling against the norm. Janet, for one, was willing to leave her first husband, an alcoholic, at a time when the word *divorce* was not accepted in polite conversation. And after she remarried and had Erica, she loved that her daughter was equally independent (even during her toddler years).

Erica and Janet were known for their many mother-daughter fun and facial moments, and these continued even when Erica left New Jersey to attend Northwestern University's acclaimed theater department. It wasn't long before Erica was pliéing with dance companies around Chicago, and after her sophomore year at school, she decided to return to the east coast and pursue her first passion, dance, full-time. In a matter of months, Erica received callbacks for shows like *A Chorus Line* and *Kiss Me, Kate.* When she joined her parents to celebrate their twenty-fifth anniversary that early November, Erica remembers thinking they had a lot to be grateful for.

It didn't seem quite real, come Thanksgiving just two weeks later, that they were dealing with the news that Janet had been diagnosed with terminal cancer. For the first time in her life, Erica was ready to *give up* the limelight and just *give to* her mom, and she took control like the toughest general around. *She* was the one who marched through the doors of the hospital everyday. *She* was the one who scoured the hallways for a tray so her mother could eat when the nurses were unable to find one. *She* was the one leading the charge of caring for her mom.

Janet passed away on February 5, less than three months after her anniversary. At her funeral, dozens of people came up to Erica and said the exact same thing: "Your mom was a best friend to me. She was always there. She always did so much." It turns out Erica and her mom had something else in common besides their independence. They both understood the importance of giving a hand . . . and they were both wholeheartedly willing to do so.

Wouldn't Your Loved Ones' Lives Be Better Places If . . .

As Anne Morrow Lindbergh said, "To give without any reward, or any notice, has a special quality of its own." One of the most beautiful things we can ever do for someone is to give to them without needing anything from them in return. Of course, it's always wonderful when someone says, "Thank you." But it's also wonderful to give without *needing* to hear anything.

A Brave, Beautiful, and Brilliant Inspiration

Love's greatest gift is its ability to make everything it touches sacred.

— BARBARA DEANGELIS

As an actress, Dana Reeve performed on Broadway, off Broadway, and in regional theaters throughout the country (she was fabulous in the production of *Brooklyn Boy* I saw in California), and she also had starring roles on television shows like *Law & Order* and *Oz*. But perhaps her greatest role began on May 27, 1995, the day her husband, Christopher Reeve of *Superman* fame, was paralyzed in a horseback riding accident.

When Christopher Reeve awoke and realized the extent of his injuries, his first thought was that maybe it would be better if he were dead. That's when Dana Reeve said, "You're still you. And I love you." For Christopher, as he shared on the Christopher and Dana Reeve Foundation Web site (*www.christopherreeve.org*), her words were "life saving."

Over the next decade, Dana Reeve did many amazing life-saving things, both for her husband and for many other people living with paralysis. She was a founding board member of the Christopher Reeve Foundation, and she established the foundation's Quality of Life grants program, which to date has given nearly $12 million to programs that improve the daily lives of people living with spinal cord injuries. Dana Reeve also did everything she could to improve her husband's quality of life up until his death in 2004, and she continued to work to help others until she passed away from lung cancer in 2006.

Dana Reeve is a particular inspiration to me, as a sibling of someone who uses a wheelchair and as the daughter of a woman who continues to do everything she can do to give my brother the best life possible. My mom has always said that what she does for my brother isn't special; it's just what needs to be done. I think the real truth is—for Dana Reeve, for my mom, for Erica, and for the many people like them who care for their loved ones—what they do is not only special, it is also sacred.

How do you want to make love your "greatest gift"?

A *Doing for My Loved Ones* Story

My mom, Sally, is someone who prefers to be behind the scenes. Even though she was an outgoing child who often danced and pranced for the cameras, as an adult she became more of an introvert. Being the person out front speaking, whether on behalf of or to other people, is not something she ever thought she would do.

After my younger brother, Gary, was born with brain damage that left him with physical and mental disabilities, my mom realized that speaking up and speaking out were two things that she was going to have to start doing . . . and she pretty much started the day Gary was born. My mom became an instant advocate for my brother, even insisting that doctors perform surgery that was required to save Gary's life when the doctors told her she should "let him die." Thirty-one years ago, at a time when most people did exactly what the doctor ordered, my mom had the courage to make a different choice for someone she loved.

Through the years, my mom has spoken up and spoken out on many occasions. She testified in front of the Maryland state legislature against a law that would have required all blind students to study Braille. As my mom says, "Braille is a wonderful tool, but it cannot help people learn when they have limited use of their hands." My mom also became president of the PTA at my sister's and my school. And she took a training course so she could become an advocate for other parents of disabled children. My mom has spoken up whenever and wherever my brother, sister, and I (and many other people) have needed her to.

Of all the things my mom has learned from her experiences, perhaps the greatest is her realization that she really can do the things she never thought she could do. While she may disagree with my opinion, I believe my mom is extraordinary. I also think that's true of *every* woman who has ever done what's needed to be done to help a loved one in need.

Wouldn't Your Loved Ones' Lives Be Better Places If . . .

Anaïs Nin once said, "Life shrinks or expands in proportion to one's courage." When our act of courage helps others, our life isn't the only life that expands. Even if a root canal seems more fun than speaking up or speaking out to you, speak up and speak out anyway. You'll be in great company with many other women who are extraordinary . . . just like you are!

What Do YOU Want to Do for Your Loved Ones?

Dr. Joyce Brothers once said, "When it comes down to it, the key to having it all is loving it all." When it comes to your loved ones, how much are you ready, willing, and able to love?

Are you ready to cancel a meeting (or hop on a plane) to spend time with someone you love, no matter how over-scheduled, overworked, or overstressed you are?

Are you willing to give to people even if their ideas of giving thanks in return are different from yours (and from Ms. Manners')? Are you willing to support people's choices wholeheartedly (and with little or no commentary) when you think their choices might land them on a "Most Stupid" list?

Are you able to be there for a friend instead of berate her if she gets you both horribly lost (be it at 2:00 p.m. or 2:00 a.m.)? Are you able to listen with no thought or concern about anything else, and no desire to compose an Oscar-worthy response (or share a Nobel Prize-worthy solution)?

If you ran the world, and had the means to do practically anything for your loved ones, what do you think they would value most? Do you think they would enjoy frequent all-expense-paid trips on your luxury jet . . . or trips on your jet when you could come, too? (Of course, teenagers may have a different answer.) Do you think they would appreciate the chance to go to all the best schools . . . or to the school of their choice? Do you think they would want a fairy-tale wedding complete with a carriage, swans, and Prince Charming . . . or the chance to marry the person they truly love (even if you think he's a toad)?

There are times when your husband, dog, best friend, and two-year-old will all vie for the top spot on your most-annoying-species list. But despite these moments, if you had the power to give your loved ones all the happiness in the world, wouldn't you want to make sure what you are giving them fits *their* definition of happiness?

Do you realize that's possible to do right now, even if you don't have a luxury jet as an accessory? As Maya Angelou says, "If you have only one smile in you, give it to the people you love." Are YOU ready, willing, and able to start today?

The Brave, Beautiful, and Brilliant
Things I Want to Do for My Loved Ones

_____

_____

_____

_____

_____

_____

_____

_____

_____

What Would You Do . . . for Your Community?

Have you ever heard about something happening in your community that made you smile more than a box of Godiva chocolates ever could?

Have you ever volunteered somewhere and been thanked for showing up and giving a hand . . . or a smile?

Have you ever been glad to have the kind of coworkers, colleagues, and neighbors that Mr. Rogers would have been proud of?

I think most everyone wants to be able to answer *Yes* to these questions. After all, who doesn't want to have the kind of neighbor who picks up the mail when you're away (or bakes you a pie when you just move in)? Who doesn't want to work with someone who is always willing to help and never needing to undermine? Who doesn't want to help a group or cause in need and know that your time (or donation) really does matter?

If you ran the world, wouldn't you do everything possible to make your communities fun, safe, and just plain great places for everyone? Wouldn't you use your newfound power so that all the stories in your local paper are the make-you-smile kind?

Barbara De Angelis once said, "Love and kindness are never wasted. They always make a difference." How would you like to use your love and kindness in your community? What kind of difference do you want to make? What would you do for your community if YOU ran the world?

10 Things You Can Do for Your Community . . . No Matter How Big or Small (the Thing or the Community)

1. Donate clothes, toys, supplies, time, money, and anything else you can think of.

2. Bake goodies for your coworkers or neighbors.

3. Buy goodies for your coworkers or neighbors if your baking (like mine) never leads to something yummy to eat.

4. Organize a fundraiser or help out the day of.

5. Say hello with a smile to everyone you see, whether you know them or not.

6. Buy a meal for someone, whether you know them or not.

7. Volunteer. Anywhere.

8. Keep the roads litter free.

9. Keep the roads rage free.

10. Welcome everyone . . . no matter what they look like, how they dress, or who they're married to.

A *Doing for My Community* Story

Ever since she can remember, Nadeen has always loved animals. And since she's often on the road for work, she's thrilled whenever she has any spare time to visit zoos around the country. A few years ago, Nadeen had the chance to explore the Columbus Zoo and Aquarium, which she had always wanted to see and always expected to love. What she didn't expect was the way her trip to that zoo would affect her.

When Nadeen was in the hallway of the aquarium, she noticed something she had never seen before: Exquisite little sea dragons that are similar in shape to the dragons of fairy-tale lore but smaller in size than her arm. Nadeen was not only amazed that, as she says, such "fantastic and magical creatures" existed but also by the fact that she did not know about them! After learning that at the time there were only three aquariums in the world with live sea dragons, Nadeen decided to combine her love of animals with her love of educating children. She decided to write her first book!

Let There Be Dragons is a wonderful and cautionary tale for kids ages four through eleven that combines fact and fiction (and is bilingual in English and Spanish). In the fiction part of the story, traditional fairy tale-type dragons are driven from the land to the sea by people who don't understand them. These dragons then evolve into the real-world sea dragons that are alive today. The book not only highlights the importance of sharing our planet, it also explains the need to take care of *all* creatures, both big and small. As a result, children learn how they can protect the real sea dragons (and their ocean habitats) that are living today.

Over the past few years, Nadeen and her publisher, Patricia Sullivan, have visited schools and have read and given the book to many children in their local community. Nadeen and Rodrigo Tobar de la Fuente (the book's very talented illustrator) have also reached out to communities around the world to spread their message. They recently gave non-exclusive publishing rights to a non-profit organization that provides ecological and reading education to villagers in Peru. Because of their efforts, people in that community are now learning about taking better care of their rivers and other natural resources.

For Nadeen, protecting animals and the environment has always been something she's loved to do but, as she also says, "You can be a passionate person even if you don't have a huge passion for just one thing." (For example, when Nadeen isn't busy educating children about the wonderful resources we can save and nurture, she loves to work with seniors and international students.) Because the real truth is, for Nadeen and for all of us, whether we help out in lots of "little" ways or focus all our time and energy on one thing, when we give in ways we truly want to, we will always make a big difference.

Wouldn't Your Communities Be Better Places If . . .

Marian Wright Edelman uttered a great truth when she said, "We must not, in trying to think about how we can make a big difference, ignore the small daily difference we can make which, over time, add up to big differences that we often cannot foresee." Whatever "small daily difference" you want to make, take Nike's advice and "Just do it." Know that even if the way you give seems small to you, it will *feel* huge to everyone and everything that benefits.

A Brave, Beautiful, and Brilliant Inspiration

Do not wait for leaders; do it alone, person to person.

— MOTHER TERESA

When Jill Buck graduated from the University of Illinois in 1991, she was commissioned as a naval officer. Besides serving as the Damage Control Instructor and the Legal, Physical Security, Admin, and Command Inspection Officer while she was stationed at Fleet Training Center in San Diego, she also gained experience with recycling programs. She is no stranger to getting things done.

That sense of initiative continued when Jill Buck moved to Pleasanton, California, and became president of the PTA. When she noticed how much waste was generated at her children's schools and how much pesticide was being sprayed near various playgrounds in her community, she decided there was something she could do to make her community safer and healthier. After inspiring the California State PTA Convention to pass a resolution regarding the harm PBTs (persistent bioaccumulative toxins) have on children, Jill Buck "realized that parents and teachers could band together to initiate substantive changes in the way communities interact with the environment for the sake of protecting children's health." She began searching for environmental education programs she could take back to her community. When she couldn't find one, she created one herself.

In July 2002, Jill Buck wrote the Go Green Initiative (*www.gogreeninitiative.org*), a "grassroots environmental program that unites parents, teachers and students to create a culture of conservation on campus." Not only does the program provide schools with simple options and tools for examining things like recycling and energy conservation, it also involves students at every level (and doesn't create extra work for teachers). By September 2002, the Go Green Initiative was being piloted at the elementary school that Jill Buck's children attended. Today it is the fastest-growing plan for helping schools become green.

Because of Jill Buck's initiative, the Go Green Initiative has been implemented in all fifty states and in schools in Africa, Asia, Canada, Europe, and Mexico, and more than one and a half million students and teachers attend and work at Go Green schools. Because of Jill Buck's contribution, her community and communities everywhere are becoming safer and healthier places, not just for children but for everyone.

When it comes to helping out in your community, what do YOU no longer want to "wait for"?

A *Doing for My Community* Story

Robin grew up as the oldest of three children, and her mom, a single parent, often remarked that Robin "was born an adult" because she took responsibility for helping around the house at an early age. Robin also helped out during the summers she lived with her father and step-mother (and six kids from three different marriages). Whether Robin was helping her mom (who was working and going to college) or keeping the peace at her dad's by cooking and cleaning to lesson her stepmother's violent outbursts, doing her part to help others in need was some-thing Robin was born to do.

As an adult, Robin has turned her desire to help others into a passion for volunteering and, as she says, she's done so much she can't even remember how she got started! What Robin does know is that she empathizes with people in need, and especially people who have been abused, because she spent a part of her childhood living with an abusive and alcoholic stepmother. One of the great organ-izations Robin has always loved working with is Habitat for Humanity, and she's done several "blitz builds," in which she has worked with a team of people—including the per-son about to become a home owner—for a week, building a house from scratch. For Robin, being able to help make that dream come true for someone has been one of the most amazing experiences around.

Through the years, Robin has done her share of walk-a-thons and bike-a-thons. She has helped at food banks, served as a volunteer coordinator for a nonprofit organization in San Francisco, and convinced her former company of three thousand employees to participate in a variety of projects (she also won the company's Humanitarian Award two years in a row). Robin has bonded with her mother during rainy weekend walks, met great friends, and introduced her husband, Ron, to the joys and satisfaction of volunteering.

For Robin, volunteering began as a way to help people overcome the same kind of struggles and challenges she faced growing up. She has met people who were experiencing extraordinary things, including homelessness, AIDS, and teenage pregnancy. Instead of feeling hopeless by the amount of help needed in her community, Robin was inspired by the amount of hope in the people she met. She also realized how much each of us really can make a difference.

Wouldn't Your Communities Be Better Places If . . .

Whoopi Goldberg once observed, "If every American donated five hours a week, it would equal the labor of 20 million full-time workers." Even if you can't imagine finding one extra hour in your week, think how much just five hours a month (or even a year) could help someone. Not only will your time and your presence make a real difference to people in your community, you can also gain quality time with your spouse or mom, meet new friends (or maybe even someone to date), and enjoy some great exercise in the process!

An Awesome Idea in Action

For most young girls, prom night is one of those evenings that we dream about and imagine for years before it actually occurs. And, as most of us remember, having the perfect prom dress is just as important as the perfect prom date. But for some girls, having any dress for the prom (let alone the perfect dress) is not an option budget-wise. Teresha Freckleton-Petite, the founder of Enchanted Closet (*www.enchantedcloset.org*), decided she wanted to change that fact for underprivileged girls in her community.

Enchanted Closet is a "volunteer-run, private non-profit service organization whose mission is to physically, mentally, and emotionally *outfit* Metro Atlanta high school girls from low-income families through programs that prepare them for social and professional milestones." The group was formed in January 2003 as a community service project to help girls attend their proms while also looking and feeling fabulous about themselves. As their Web site says, "No high school girl should miss this rite of passage because she could not afford a dress." The group received tremendous support and hundreds of incredible gowns from many places throughout the Atlanta community. Since that first fundraising drive, Enchanted Closet has given away nearly 1,600 prom dresses, 100 homecoming dresses, and more than 100 dresses for other important occasions.

For the founders of Enchanted Closet, the connection between clothing and self-esteem provides "an opportunity to empower young girls." Recently, they have expanded their ability to help young girls in their community by offering both life readiness workshops and clothing for college and job interviews. As the founders realized, they are "in a unique position to make a positive difference in the lives of young girls." They are also committed to making a positive difference in as many ways as they possibly can.

Here's an Idea You Can Do for Your Community
Today . . .
Check out *www.enchantedcloset.org* to learn more about the programs this great group of women have created, or to get ideas for starting an Enchanted Closet program or holding an Enchanted Closet fundraising drive in your community.

A *Doing for My Community* Story

Aly was born in Mexicali and moved to the United States when she was thirteen years old. No matter where she's lived, Aly has always been someone who likes to smile at others. She likes to, as she says, "focus on the positive." That sentiment helped her when her husband passed away just five months after she gave birth to their son. Though some of her family was living in Texas, Aly had no family nearby in California. She decided she would make her community and, in particular, her community at work, her second family.

Aly began working at her job in 2005, and she was impressed by how many others had been at the company (a custom optical manufacturing company with twenty employees) for fifteen years or more. Aly decided she wanted to add to the wonderful environment at her new job, and she started bringing in fun surprises right away. Aly regularly leaves flowers on people's desks just to make them smile (and without any prompting from a holiday or birthday). And when she brings in goodies for the snack table (something she does often), she doesn't just leave them there. Instead, she delivers her treats in person, stopping by *everyone*'s desk so she can say hello and ask how they are. Aly is always that person who will listen . . . and who really cares.

In fact, the special things Aly does for others are not limited to food and flowers, or to people in her work community. Not long ago, when Aly learned one of her coworkers did not have enough money to visit her mom who was sick in Mexico, Aly explained the situation to her other coworkers and together they raised the travel money for their colleague. Outside of work, Aly has helped a drug addict get clean, a homeless friend return home, and she has begun volunteering at a hospital after work. For Aly, it's important to offer comfort to people who need it, even if she is extra-tired some nights when she gets home.

Aly's boss, Julie, suggested her for this story, much to Aly's shock and surprise. Aly never realized anyone (especially her boss) noticed all the things that feel so natural for her to do. Not only have *all* her coworkers noticed, they see Aly as "an amazing morale lift." Because of Aly, people in her work community not only have yummy birthday potlucks and great ice cream during the summer, they also regularly spend time together (both bosses and employees, men and women, of many different cultures). The things that Aly does for her coworkers bring everyone, as Julie says, "to the same level." They also bring the kind of camaraderie and togetherness all communities deserve.

Wouldn't Your Communities Be Better Places If . . .

Mother Teresa once said, "Let no one come to you without leaving better and happier." The great thing about that notion: you don't need to wait for people to come to you. Whether you live, work, or play in a community of 5 or 500,000, go out and do something—*anything*—to make your community better and happier. You may not think anyone will notice, but as Aly learned, people do notice, and they are affected in ways we sometimes never imagine.

The *Better and Happier* Pact

To my neighbors, friends, and colleagues ... (and everyone else nearby):

From this day forward, I want to do my part to make our community the best and happiest it can be. I know there may be days when I ...

❋ Honk at you ... or maybe even make a hand gesture

❋ Drop something ... and don't stop to pick it up

❋ Forget most people like to sleep at 3:00 a.m. ... or remember but blast U2 or Dave Matthews Band anyway

❋ Care about a deadline ... and forget to care about your feelings

❋ Feel grouchy, cranky, irritable, and exhausted ... and completely take it out on you

I will do my best to make these days as short, infrequent, and shout-free as possible! I'll also apologize (or grovel) about them whenever I need to!

Name _____ Date _____

A *Doing for My Community* Story

Shannon has always been someone who has loved helping children. As a little girl, she knew she wanted to grow up and be a teacher, and she started baby-sitting as soon as she was old enough to do so. Shannon began teaching first grade in 2000 and, during her summer break in 2005, she watched in horror as Hurricane Katrina devastated the Gulf Coast. Shannon knew she wanted to do something for the children who lost not just their homes but also their schools and communities. She was given an opportunity to help during her school's "Back to School" week, when she learned that her school in suburban Maryland was "adopting" an elementary school in Mississippi.

Shannon knew immediately that she wanted to play a large part in her school's efforts. She spoke to the other first grade team members at her school and asked if they wanted to "adopt" the first graders at the school in Mississippi. Everyone did, and Shannon contacted the first grade teachers in Mississippi to see what they needed (snacks, books, and school supplies were the top items). Shannon then drafted a letter asking for donations and sent it home to all the first grade families at her school. It wasn't long before things like pretzels, Dr. Seuss books, and crayons came piling in. Shannon and the other teachers also donated everything from teacher's workbooks to stickers to the Mississippi teachers.

Shannon's desire to help her adopted class didn't stop once the school year was in full swing. She kept in touch with the first grade teachers to see how things were going, and she regularly asked them if they needed anything. Around the holidays, her class sent another huge shipment of goodies to the first graders and teachers in Mississippi. Shannon also asked the first grade teachers if they wanted to attend the Spring Fest at her school that spring. Although the teachers were unable to come, they wanted to allow a family from their school to represent them and receive part of the Spring Fest proceeds in person.

The family selected by the Mississippi teachers had lost almost everything in the hurricane and had spent time living in horrible conditions in tents and on a cruise ship before finally settling into a one-bedroom apartment and then a rental house. Through everything the family experienced, the mom was helping the school a great deal and the teachers really appreciated her. Shannon spent hours searching for flights for the family and gathered donations from her fellow teachers and the PTA to pay for the tickets. She also convinced a local hotel to donate a suite for the family to stay in, organized a sightseeing day for the family with a family from her class, and purchased tickets for the family to attend the Spring Fest (where both Shannon and the family from Mississippi were honored by Maryland's governor).

Shannon still keeps in touch with the family who visited. As she says, "We were strangers who may have never met and now we are lifelong friends." Because the real truth is, for Shannon and for all of us, one of the best things about helping others is that it's one of the best ways we can expand our community of friends.

Wouldn't Your Communities Be Better Places If . . .

Shirley MacLaine once observed, "The more I traveled the more I realized that fear makes strangers of people who should be friends." If there's an organization, group, or cause that you want to join or help, get involved today, even (and especially) if you don't know anyone there. Not only will people welcome your help, they'll be touched that you would want to befriend them.

A Brave, Beautiful, and Brilliant Inspiration

Some people give time, some money, some their skills and connections, some literally give their life's blood . . . but everyone has something to give.

— BARBARA BUSH

Oral Lee Brown was born in the Mississippi Delta, and even though she grew up in poverty, she was fortunate to have a supportive family who taught her how important it is to give to others. The significance of both family and giving back stayed with Oral Lee Brown when she moved to California and worked during the day while attending the University of San Francisco at night. After she graduated, Oral Lee Brown loved raising her three daughters and serving on community boards as much as she loved working, first in management and then as a real estate agent and restaurant owner.

One morning in 1987, Oral Lee Brown had an experience that changed not only her life but the lives of some first graders living nearby. When she popped into a store near her office in Oakland to buy snacks for work, a little girl asked her for a quarter, but instead of buying candy, the little girl purchased bread and bologna for her family. Oral Lee Brown kept wondering why the little girl was trying to find food for her family instead of attending school, so she visited a local elementary school, and even though she didn't see the little girl, she did see twenty-three other first graders. That's when Oral Lee Brown pledged that she would pay for every single first grader to attend college if he or she graduated high school. At the time, Oral Lee Brown earned $45,000 a year.

Oral Lee Brown started the Oral Lee Brown Foundation and pledged to donate $10,000 each year to pay for the first graders' college tuition. Through her own perseverance, and with the eventual help of corporate donations, Oral Lee Brown kept her promise and sent nineteen of the original twenty-three first graders to college (with the first one graduating college in 2003). In recent years, Oral Lee Brown once again promised new groups of students that she would pay college tuition for each student who graduated high school. I'd say it's no surprise that Oral Lee Brown was recently selected by CNN *Heroes* (a program that honors ordinary people doing extraordinary things) as a wonderful example of someone who champions children.

On her foundation's Web site (*www.oralleebrownfoundation.com*), Oral Lee Brown says, "If these children become successful, then my life will have been a success. After this, I will look forward to helping others." For the children in Oral Lee Brown's community, her "something to give" has been life changing not just for them, but for everyone they themselves will now be able to affect.

What "something" do YOU want to give?

A *Doing for My Community* Story

Throughout her life, family has always been important to Judee. Growing up, she was close to her parents, and when she lived in Northern California for thirteen years as an adult, she really missed them. Now that she's in her early sixties and back in Southern California, Judee loves the fact that she lives right next door to her parents (even more than she loves the ocean view they share), and that both of her daughters, her grandchildren, and some cousins, aunts, and uncles live just a few miles away.

For Judee's family, the holidays are always a fun time, filled with great food, great fun, and great music (the Dixie Chicks and the Rolling Stones are always favorites). One year just before Thanksgiving, Judee's daughter Julie became friends with a Marine named Richard who was stationed in nearby Camp Pendleton. When Judee learned that Richard would be away from his family for the holidays for the first time, she invited him to spend both Thanksgiving and Christmas with her family. He did, and the tradition of "Inviting the Marines for the Holidays" was born.

Through the years, Judee's family has opened their home to Marines from Washington, Oregon, Nevada, Oklahoma, Idaho, and North Carolina, among others. Judee and her daughters, Julie and Cari, have driven by Marines they'd never met who were calling home from a phone booth (in the not-so-long-ago days when phone booths were still common) and invited them home for Thanksgiving dinner. As Judee remembers, their faces turned from puzzled to absolute delight, especially when they drove through the gates leading to Judee's house and smelled the amazing food cooking inside. Not only did the Marines enjoy a great dinner, but Judee let them use her home phone to call their own families. Some years, the Marines spent their entire four-day leave with Judee or another member of her family instead of returning to base after dinner.

To this day, Judee is still in touch with many of the Marines she met. Judee's mom, June, wrote to the Marines where they were stationed, and Judee recently visited one Marine named Brian and his wife, Barbara, in Tampa, Florida. She's even been to Richard's wedding in California and Brian's wedding in Nevada!

Judee always says, "No one should ever have to be alone during the holidays." Through the years, Judee and her family have not only given the Marines a great meal and some great laughs, they've also given them (and everyone they've ever invited over, myself included), the wonderful feeling of home and belonging. Because the real truth is, when we let it, our sense of community does not have to be bound by any limits or walls at all.

Wouldn't Your Communities Be Better Places If . . .

Mother Teresa once said, "Loneli-ness is the most terrible poverty." Consider opening your home to someone from your community like Judee has, during the holidays or even on a Saturday night (and you don't need to find a phone booth first). If you look closely among your acquaintances, colleagues, or coworkers, you'll find more than one person who would be honored to accept.

An Awesome Idea in Action

Did you know that . . .

According to the Making Memories Breast Cancer Association (*www.makingmemories.org*),

❋ In the United States alone, one person will be diagnosed with breast cancer every 2 1/2 minutes?

❋ Nearly 40,000 people in the United States (and more than 300,000 people worldwide) are expected to die from breast cancer this year?

❋ Breast cancer is the second highest killer of women in the United States, and the number one killer of U.S. women between ages 15 and 54?

Fran Hansen and her daughter, Anna Nelson, learned the scary statistics about breast cancer after Fran had a personal breast cancer scare in 1997 and wanted to find out everything she possibly could while she was waiting for her test results. While Fran was ultimately diagnosed as cancer-free, she kept thinking about all the letters and stories she had read of both women and men whose diagnoses were different than hers. Fran and Anna decided they wanted to help people struggling with breast cancer, so they founded the Making Memories Breast Cancer Foundation as a result.

The Making Memories Breast Cancer Foundation is not only committed to spreading awareness and education about breast cancer and available resources for the disease, it also provides "an opportunity for metastatic breast cancer patients' dream or wish to be fulfilled by providing a special time of 'Making Memories' together with their families." Besides creating the Brides Against Breast Cancer(™) fundraising program (*www.bridesagainstbreastcancer.org*), now with more than thirty-two bridal shows around the country each year, the foundation has also created the Pink Envelope Project(™) (*www.pinkenvelopeproject.org*) to make it easy for everyone, from individuals to groups and companies to students, to plan a fundraiser in their community.

A Pink Envelope Project™ can be "any personal fundraiser centered around an event, gathering, party, activity, or club that you attend or host." The Web site provides great activity ideas for individuals (scrap-booking parties and bridal showers, to name two) and businesses (charity galas and golf tournaments, to name two more) alike, as well as a community area where members can share suggestions, post photos from their events, and pay tribute to loved ones. There is no cost to join the Pink Envelope Project™, only a willingness to help the project educate the public and become the biggest fundraising arm for the Making Memories Breast Cancer Foundation.

Fran Hansen and Anna Nelson began the Making Memories Breast Cancer Foundation and the Pink Envelope Project™ because they "imagine a world where compassionate individuals, organizations, companies and corporations unite with the common goal of providing a moment of calm for a family amidst the hurricane of disease and financial constrains." Isn't that a great vision communities everywhere can share?

Here's an Idea You Can Do for Your Community *Today* . . . Check out *www.pinkenvelopeproject.org* to learn more about hosting a Pink Envelope Project™ fundraiser in your community. Whether you are motivated to help because of a personal experience or just because, if you are motivated, then why not get started today?

A *Doing for My Community* Story

Leslie grew up as an only child, and she was raised by just her mom from the time she was four years old. Leslie's mom was a fourth grade teacher, and she made as much of an impact on her daughter as she did on her students (not long ago, a former student, now in his forties, tracked Leslie down so that he could tell her how much her mom had influenced him). That didn't surprise Leslie at all, since Leslie's mom was always her number one supporter. Leslie and her mom never went through that awkward door-slamming, always-yelling-at-each-other period. They preferred to giggle, act goofy, and have fun. They truly had a great relationship.

Leslie's mom died suddenly when Leslie was sixteen years old, and as Leslie says her world "was turned upside down." For years, Leslie felt damaged, like she was wearing a kind of scarlet letter that separated her from the rest of the world. It wasn't until she was in college and read the book *Motherless Daughters* by Hope Edelman that she realized other people knew how she felt.

As time went on, Leslie met other women whose moms had passed away, and they appreciated meeting someone like Leslie, who understood the depth of loss they were feeling. One day, around twelve years after her mom had died, Leslie overheard a woman in Macy's jewelry department say that she had just lost her mom. When Leslie approached the woman and said, "I've been through it and I understand," the woman started to cry . . . and then she started to talk. For the first time, Leslie realized how much she could help other women who had lost their moms (even if she just listened to them share their stories). Leslie also realized she didn't feel sad doing so.

In 2004, Leslie started the Mamma Mia Sisterhood, so that women who had lost their mothers would no longer feel alone. An event planner by trade, Leslie has loved organizing get-togethers like guest speakers, trivia night at Mellow Mushroom pizza, museum trips, and tea at the Ritz-Carlton the day before Mother's Day (which happens to be International Motherless Daughters Day). The Mamma Mia Sisterhood now has more than 100 members who, in varying numbers, meet once a month. They uplift each other. They support each other. And they remind each other that they are not on their own.

Leslie will tell you that one of the things she loved most about her mom was her mom's generosity and commitment to making a difference in other people's lives. In that regard, Leslie's mom inspired the Mamma Mia Sisterhood in the best way possible: now Leslie is carrying on the family tradition of having an impact on others.

Wouldn't Your Communities Be Better Places If . . .

Perhaps Anne Frank said it best when she said, "Don't think of all the misery but of all the beauty that still remains." Each of us can use the events that shape our lives to help others who are experiencing the same thing. Whether we gather people together or just listen when someone needs to talk, we can remind each other how great and beautiful life (and some shared chocolate, pizza, and fun trivia) can be.

An Awesome Idea in Action

Did you know that . . .
   According to the American Heart Association,

❋ Sudden cardiac death from coronary heart disease
   occurs over 900 times per day in the United States?

❋ Approximately 95 percent of sudden cardiac arrest
   victims die before reaching the hospital?

❋ Effective bystander CPR, provided immediately
   after cardiac arrest, can double a victim's chance
   of survival?

For Linette Derminer of Ohio, Rachel Moyer of
Pennsylvania, Sharon Bates of Arizona, and Laura Friend
of Texas, these statistics are personal. Each of these women
has lost a child to sudden cardiac arrest—losses that could
have been prevented through early detection, education,
awareness, and/or proper placement of automated external
defibrillators (AEDs). They decided to form the Parent
Heart Watch (*www.parentheartwatch.org*) to effect change
"so young people can have a second chance at life."

Parent Heart Watch is a "state-by-state network of
parents dedicated to reducing the often disastrous effects
of Sudden Cardiac Arrest (SCA) in children." The organization and families involved have changed laws, held

screening events, and placed thousands of AEDs in and around their communities. Check out their "Defibrillator Program," which helps people place AEDs in public places, and their "Make the Grade" program, which helps parents place AEDs in schools.

The sad truth is that 90 to 95 percent of all sudden cardiac arrest victims die. The great truth is that they don't have to! As Parent Heart Watch shares in the Sudden Cardiac Arrest section of their Web site, "Survival rates can rise to 70 percent or more when an AED program is in place." What's more, "sixth-grade school children with moderate training can learn to use AEDs to save the lives of cardiac arrest victims almost as quickly and efficiently as professional emergency medical personnel."

Parent Heart Watch was inspired by the losses four mothers experienced and their subsequent commitment to "take action that can protect other children." The organization is a testament to what we can do as individuals and as a group of people at the local, state, and national community levels.

Here's an Idea You Can Do for Your Community *Today* . . . Check out *www.parentheartwatch.org* to get educated and learn more about setting up AED programs in your community. Help this great organization protect children in communities everywhere.

A *Doing for My Community* Story

Patty has always been someone who has believed in giving back to her community. As she says, giving to others and helping people, especially when there is a need, gives her "deep soul satisfaction." Sharing is something she can never imagine *not* doing.

One of the ways Patty has always enjoyed contributing has been volunteering at what is now the Laguna College of Art & Design, located in beautiful Laguna Beach, California. Even as a super-busy realtor (she was the number two realtor from Los Angeles to San Diego for her company one year and a consistent top producer for many of her twenty-eight years there), Patty always made time to help out at the college (besides serving on the board of the college, she joined Designing Women, the college's support arm). What's more, *she* felt immense gratitude for the education and understanding of both art and beauty that she received in the process.

When fires devastated parts of her beach community, Patty and other members of Designing Women and the college community rallied to help people who lost their homes. The organization sponsored an Art Day for the fire victims and anyone else affected by the fires, either physically or emotionally. Art therapy helped people who had lost everything create new memories and new treasures for the new homes they would build one day. Patty remembers a mother and her two daughters who began to replace their handmade Christmas decorations that were lost in the fire with new ones they made during the Art Day. As Patty says, it was wonderful to see them create a "new family tradition and forward their own inner healing."

Through her experiences helping her community after the fires (she also participated in the distribution of clothing donations and helped find people housing), Patty learned that in the midst of tragedy people care less about their differences and more about making sure those in need are kindly taken care of. Because the truth is, when we help others, we never have less than we would have had otherwise. Instead, we gain more than we imagine is possible. To quote Patty directly, "I have been so enriched by the time and energy I have freely given that it has returned to me in deeper connections, heightened awareness, and lovely friendships."

Wouldn't Your Communities Be Better Places If . . .

Eleanor Roosevelt once said, "When you cease to make a contribution, you begin to die." I think she would also agree that when you choose to make a contribution, especially in a time of urgency, you give everyone involved a second chance at life.

> If there is ever a tragedy in your community, know that whatever you have to give is valuable, beautiful, and always enough.

What Do YOU Want to Do for Your Community?

Bertha Von Suttner, the first woman to win the Nobel Peace Prize, once said, "After the verb 'to Love,' 'to Help' is the most beautiful verb in the world." When it comes to your community, how do you want to help or to love?

Do you want to volunteer like Robin does, help out in lots of little ways like Nadeen, or open your home to others like Judee? Have you been inspired by something in your personal life, like Leslie, or were you ready to contribute during a tragedy like Patty? Are you ready to experience the joy of meeting new friends, like Shannon, or the satisfaction you'll receive from making things better and happier, like Aly?

Think about it: What really inspires you? What do you lose sleep over or dream of? What are you unable to stop talking or wondering about (or standing on a soapbox for)?

If you ran the world . . . and had unlimited access to resources (both the people and the paper kind) . . . you could immediately and single-handedly make each of your communities a better place. Whether you wanted to hold a book drive in your neighborhood, create a family fun day at your office, or help runaways, the homeless, or anyone else who ends up on your streets, you would have everything you needed at the snap of a finger to put your awesome ideas into immediate action. The great thing is, choosing to help out in your communities *today* and in *any way*, no matter the size of your resources or amount of time you have available, is just as important (and even more amazing, since more than a finger snap or two is required).

Jodie Foster once said, "Let how you live your life stand for something, no matter how small and incidental it may seem." When how you live your life stands for making your communities better places, there is nothing small or incidental about it, especially to the person or people you touch. Is there someone you want to affect? Is there something you want your life to stand for? Is there a way you want to give back to your communities?

Whether you are already giving in the ways that matter most to you, or you are still figuring out what that means, the great thing is that you never have to live up to anyone else's deadline or dollar amounts. Each of us can make a beautiful difference in our own unique and beautiful way. The only question to answer is: **What kind of beautiful difference do YOU want to make?**

The Brave, Beautiful, and Brilliant Things I Want to Do for My Community

_____

_____

_____

_____

_____

_____

_____

_____

_____

What Would You Do . . . for the World?

Have you ever sent food, money, or clothing to people somewhere in the world whom you have never met?

Have you ever wanted to hop on a plane (or actually boarded one) so you could meet those people . . . and help them yourself?

Have you ever heard a news story that contained words like *gunfire, war, starvation, poverty, violence, rape, disease, flooding, tsunami,* or *ethnic cleansing* and thought, "I know we can do better than this!"

With all the things that are happening in the world, most of us feel a longing to help when and where help is needed. Most of us would gladly do whatever we can to make the poverty and war news stories a thing of the past. And most of us have spent time wondering, "What is it that *I* can personally do? How can *I* make a difference?"

If you ran the world, and had the means and ability to do pretty much *any*thing, how would you help when pretty much *any* kind of help was possible? How would you get started? What would you do first, second, and third? How about fourth, fifth, and sixth?

Marian Wright Edelman said, "If you don't like the way the world is, you change it. You have an obligation to change it. You just do it one step at a time." How do you want to change the world? What steps do you want to take? What would you do for the world if YOU ran the world?

10 Things You Can Do for the World . . . No Matter Where You Are

1. Show children everywhere that helping others is important at every age.

2. Show children everywhere that sharing is important at every age.

3. Understand (and help other people understand) that our world's natural resources are *not* unlimited.

4. Reduce, Reuse, and Recycle whatever you can.

5. Listen to other people's perspectives.

6. Accept and *allow* other people's perspectives, especially when they are vastly different than yours.

7. See the world in color, not in black and white.

8. Forgive someone (or some nation) for something, especially things that feel unforgivable.

9. Value everyone you meet.

10. Value everyone . . . even if you never meet.

A *Doing for the World* Story

For as long as she can remember, learning about other places has been a regular part of Jyn's life. Her maternal grandparents adopted her uncle from Thailand and regularly hosted foreign exchange students in their home. Her paternal grandparents and her aunt and uncle were international missionaries who shared tales with Jyn from practically every continent in the world. Jyn herself took her first steps on foreign soil when she was three years old and her father took her with him to an orphanage in Mexico (the first of many trips like that). From an early age, Jyn caught the travel bug, developing a passion for cultures, countries, and continents everywhere.

Through the years, Jyn's travels have taken her around the world and back again, and her experiences have been as varied as they have been amazing. When Jyn was thirteen years old, she braved the jungles of Indonesia without her parents for an entire summer as part of a teen mission group. Instead of staying in a camp with bunk beds and showers, political turmoil forced her group to camp in tents and bathe in a river that had, as Jyn remembers, "leeches—but they wouldn't stick to you if you moved fast enough." The following summer, Jyn traveled to Poland (just as the country was transitioning from Communist rule) where she sang on the Promenade and brought smiles to many faces. And before she graduated high school, Jyn traveled to France, Luxemburg, Belgium, and Ireland (and enjoyed having a wonderful crush on an Irish boy and an even more wonderful crush on a British boy), spent time learning mime with street performers in Spain, visited the Wailing Wall in Jerusalem, and hiked the Swiss Alps. Even though she had some scary travel moments (like close calls with her health and missing two terrorist bombings by a matter of days), she never once regretted her choices to see more of the world we live in.

Recently, Jyn was able to combine her acting chops with her love of international cultures by starring in a wonderful educational DVD for preschool- and elementary-aged kids called *Baku the Travel Bug*, which is about helping children everywhere make friends around the world (and which won the prestigious Parents' Choice Approved Award and garnered mentions in magazines like *Parenting* and *Scholastic Parent & Child*). In the program, neighborhood children visit Jyn's character, Aunt Sydney, and her puppet friend Baku (an adorable blue and yellow bug) who share their magical scrapbook filled with pictures that come to life from their adventures all over the world. Children are introduced to kids from other countries who teach them how to do things like make tostadas and dance Lebanese style. As Jyn says, she's loved being part of a project that helps kids learn about other cultures at the same age she did. She also enjoys hearing stories about young Baku viewers who now like to play dress-up in a sari, say hello in several languages, and are fascinated by maps and globes.

Jyn has met many people from many different places in her life, but there is one thing she has always found to be true: people's prejudices and stereotypes have a wonderful way of disappearing when they meet each other one on one and realize that, as Jyn always says, "We're all just people. We laugh. We cry. And we have more in common than we realize." Imagine what would happen to the world if that was the lesson people everywhere learned from the moment they were born.

Wouldn't the World Be a Better Place If . . .

Maya Angelou once said, "Perhaps travel cannot prevent bigotry, but by demonstrating that all people cry, laugh, eat, worry, and die, it can introduce the idea that if we try and understand each other, we may even become friends." Whether you actually travel the world like Jyn or learn about other places via the World Wide Web, you can choose to see the world (and teach others to see the world) as an extraordinary place filled with friends instead of a place with enemies to fear. You can also realize that an entire culture is not responsible (and should not be hated) for the actions certain individuals take.

A Brave, Beautiful, and Brilliant Inspiration

You really *can* change the world if you care enough.

— MARIAN WRIGHT EDELMAN

Dame Anita Roddick started The Body Shop in 1976, and from the very beginning, when the company was just one tiny store in Brighton, England, she was committed to running a business that supported both the environment and human rights. Taking a lesson from her mother's actions during World War II, Dame Anita Roddick insisted that the company reuse everything, refill everything, and recycle as much as they could. She also believed that all of their products should be "made with a love of life, respect for the world we live in, a spirit of individuality, and commitment to trading fairly."

Dame Anita Roddick opened a second store within six months, and the first overseas franchise opened two years later. By 1985, The Body Shop became a public company, and in 2008 the company (now known as The Body Shop International) has more than 2,100 stores in 55 countries. At every stage of the company's growth, Dame Anita Roddick insisted that the company honor five values: Protect Our Planet, Support Community Trade, Against Animal Testing, Defend Human Rights, and Activate Self

Esteem. As it says on *www.thebodyshopinternational.com*, "To us, there is no other way to work. After all, when you believe in what you do, you do it better."

Through the years, Dame Anita Roddick and The Body Shop have supported many important causes and campaigns, including Greenpeace, Save the Whales, Stopping Violence in the Home, Human and Sexual Trafficking, Ending Global Warming, and many others. The company was the first international cosmetics brand to win the Humane Cosmetics Standard for their Against Animal Testing policy, and they are also the only cosmetics company with an extensive commitment to fair trade (in fact, they have their own fair trade program called Community Trade, which now works with "31 suppliers in 24 countries, providing over 15,000 people across the globe with essential income to build their futures"). And the Body Shop Foundation was founded in 1990 as a charitable trust to support "innovative global projects working in the areas of human & civil rights and environmental & animal protection." To date, the foundation has donated more than £11 million in grants to charities working to change the planet for the better (recent recipients include Amazon Rainforest Foundation, Navdanya Trust [a pioneer of the organic movement in India], Change for Children Association [a supporter of sustainable community development in Latin America, Africa, and the Caribbean] and many others).

Dame Anita Roddick has been given many well-deserved honors and awards through the years, including the Center for World Development Education's World Vision Award in 1991, a medal from the National Audubon Society in 1993, the United Nations Environment Programme Honouree for Eyes on the Environment in 1997, the International Peace Prayer Day Organization's Woman of Peace in 2001, and she was named a Dame Commander of the British Empire in 2003. Sadly, Dame Anita Roddick passed away in September 2007. One of the things she had written on her Web site, *www.anitaroddick.com*, is, "Businesses have the power to do good. That's why The Body Shop's mission statement opens with the overriding commitment, 'To dedicate our business to the pursuit of social and environmental change.'" What a wonderful mission for all businesses . . . and for all of us!

How do YOU want to "change the world"?

A *Doing for the World* Story

Andrea is one of those people who has always loved nature. As a little girl, her family would often spend Sundays bird watching, and she remembers being mesmerized by the roadrunners that would speed down the country rode where she grew up in Texas. Andrea also watched her mom conserve by doing things like carrying cloth bags and collecting rain water. For Andrea, reusing, reducing, and recycling was her way of life long before "going green" was something people talked about.

When Andrea was diagnosed with a life-threatening autoimmune disease that caused her immune system to begin attacking her muscles, she knew she needed to do something before her heart was affected. From everything she learned about the environment as a child, she knew that exposure to toxins could be directly affecting her health. At a friend's suggestion, Andrea began taking vitamins and using natural, nontoxic, phosphate-free cleaning products made by a company called Shaklee (*www.shaklee.com*), a health and wellness company that has been in business for more than fifty years and whose products are made to be entirely in harmony with nature. In a matter of weeks, everyone who saw Andrea told her that they could see life again in her eyes. More important, Andrea felt great for the first time in a long time.

As Andrea has switched all her household cleaning products to ones that are completely nontoxic, she has lived completely free of any traces of the disease that had once threatened her life. Recently, when Andrea was at a seminar, she decided she wanted to use her personal experience to help people and the planet in a real and measurable way. She knew from her own life that Shaklee's Get Clean(™) Starter Kit (which contains nontoxic versions of all the household cleaners people use and need) could help people feel better (and even possibly save people's lives). She also knew that each kit keeps 108 pounds of packaging waste out of landfills and eliminates 248 pounds of greenhouse gases because the products are concentrated.

At first, Andrea set a goal of selling 1,000 kits, but the more she thought about it, the more she knew that goal would be easy to reach given all the people she knew. That's when Andrea decided she could do more. She decided to set a goal of selling 10,000 kits, which would reduce the amount of garbage going into our landfills by more than one million pounds (and help even more people live healthier and feel better)! And she's already made great progress through her Web site, *www.shaklee.net/andrea_hylen*.

Since Andrea set her goal of selling 10,000 kits in July 2007, she has been educating people everywhere possible, from state fairs to career fairs to networking meetings. She has also had a little help from Oprah, who recently named Shaklee's Get Clean(™) Starter Kit as one of her favorite things. Andrea always says, "The choices we make create our world." I know she also agrees that if each of us chooses wisely, our actions will help us save the planet.

Wouldn't the World Be a Better Place If . . .

Rachel Carson once said, "The human race is challenged more than ever before to demonstrate our mastery—not over nature but of ourselves." However you feel comfortable reusing, reducing, or recycling (be it taking shorter showers, using energy-efficient light bulbs, taking cloth bags to the grocery store, or one of the many other great ways you can conserve), don't wait another day to start. If everyone does just one thing, that alone could possibly prevent the level of devastation recent hurricanes, tsunamis, and fires have caused. Isn't our future, and our children's future, at least worthy of the attempt?

An Awesome Idea in Action

Did you know that . . .

According to information gathered by Pump 'Em Up (*www.pumpemup.org*) from the U.S. Department of Energy, the U.S. Department of Transportation, Michelin, Firestone, and Goodyear, with properly inflated tires,

❊ Americans could save hundreds of dollars each year on gasoline and extend the life of their tires by 25 percent?

❊ Americans could protect the Arctic National Wildlife Refuge (the largest wildlife refuge in the United States, whose 19 million acres are home to millions of migratory birds, caribou, polar bears, grizzly bears, black bears, wolves, and many other species) *forever?*

❊ Americans could help stop global warming by burning less gas and lowering emissions?

Savannah Walters learned these facts in 2001 when she was in the second grade and had several experiences that made her want to do something to help the environment. That year, she learned all about the Arctic in school, and she became worried about what would happen to the animals, trees, and other beautiful elements of Alaska's Arctic National Wildlife Refuge if the proposals to drill for oil there were allowed to move forward. She and her family also visited the Grand Canyon, where she took a Junior Rangers course that included an oath to protect the environment *and* teach others to do so as well.

After her mother saw a photo exhibit about the Arctic by long-time environmental activist Lenny Kohm, Savannah Walters called him and he explained that Americans waste four million gallons of gas every day by driving on under-inflated tires. What's more, we would actually save "as much oil as would be produced by the new drilling if drivers simply pumped up their car tires to proper inflation levels." That's when Savannah Walters asked, "Why would we keep on wasting gas and looking for more when we could easily just pump 'em up?" And when Savannah Walters learned that properly inflated tires lower car emissions, which are the second largest contributing factor to global warming, she decided it was time to take action. Pump 'Em Up! was born as a result.

Pump 'Em Up! is "a fuel conservation call to all over the world to spread the word to drivers that the power to conserve fuel is in their own tires!" The Web site contains all the information people need to learn how to properly inflate their tires and to create Pump 'Em Up chapters in communities all over the world. Visitors can also download flyers to put on cars parked at participating schools and community groups to inspire people to get involved.

Recently, Savannah Walters was profiled on the CNN *Heroes* program for the extraordinary things she has done for the environment. In her interview, she said, "It's just about protecting the planet and wanting to live in a clean world." How can any of us argue with that?

Here's an Idea You Can Do for the World *Today* . . . Check out *www.pumpemup.org* to learn more about how to make sure your tires are properly inflated, and then take a few moments each month to do just that. Not only will you save money, you will help save the planet in the process!

A *Doing for the World* Story

Mary has always been a natural at telling stories. Whether she was entertaining her younger sister Hannah (who was born when Mary was ten) or an audience of hundreds during one of the many plays she's been in, Mary believes that there are many important stories that she can share with the world. Mary especially wants to be a voice for people everywhere whose stories aren't being heard, including children whose voices, as Mary says, are often the first to be ignored.

Given Mary's passion for performing, it's no surprise that in 2006 she jumped at the chance to help other actors found a new theater company called Dramatic Adventure Theatre (*www.dramaticadventure.com*). The theater's mission is to provide "the opportunity for artists to perform around the world, to explore the unknown and the familiar, and to become intimately involved with distant communities in order to build a platform where ideas, talent, and original works can be shared." Their first project: to team with Forgotten Voices International, a nonprofit organization that helps AIDS orphans in southern Africa, and give children from Zimbabwe a voice by sending a team of New York-based actors to Africa so they could perform plays the children had written.

When a severe drought in late 2006 and early 2007 forced many of the local Zimbabwe teens to leave school with plays unfinished, Mary and her fellow actors traveled to Zimbabwe anyway that summer and provided time for many students to complete their plays. *Voices from Zimbabwe* is now a full-length play, with 90 percent of the content directly written by children and teens from Zimbabwe (the actors from Dramatic Adventure also wrote a handful of monologues based on their experiences in Africa that are included in the play, too). The play has already been performed in several cities throughout the United States. What's more, the Dramatic Adventure troupe will to return to Zimbabwe in 2008 to write a new play that will be performed by the Bulawayo Young Company (a theater company that gives a voice to many of Zimbabwe's talented young actors). The actors from Dramatic Adventure are also planning a trip to Ecuador in 2008 to help give children there a voice for their unique (and sometimes harrowing) experiences.

I think one of the most amazing things Mary said about her trip to Zimbabwe is, "If you read any of the stories written by the kids in Africa, you would never know they grew up in a different country unless they said so. We really are more alike than we realize." Another amazing thing Mary said: "Whatever language we speak to children is the language they learn." Through Dramatic Adventure Theatre, Mary wants to help spread the language of peace, understanding, and appreciation of differences. She also wants the world to realize that children are our most valuable resource, one we cannot continue to neglect, undervalue, or ignore.

Wouldn't the World Be a Better Place If . . .

Margaret Atwood said, "A voice is a human gift; it should be cherished and used, to utter as fully human speech as possible." This statement is true for every voice, regardless of age, gender, or geography. Think of it this way: children who use their voices to express peace and understanding become adults who use their voices to express peace and understanding. When we listen to these children . . . and help their voices be heard by as many people as possible . . . we help them create the beautiful future they deserve.

An Awesome Idea in Action

Did you know that . . .

According to findings reported in the Trafficking Victims Protection Reauthorization Act of 2005,

※ As many as 300,000 children in the United States are at risk for commercial sexual exploitation, including trafficking, at any given time?

※ An estimated 600,000 to 800,000 individuals are trafficked across international borders each year and exploited through forced labor and commercial sex exploitation?

※ Of all the people who are trafficked each year, an estimated 80 percent are women and children?

Linda Smith may not have known these specific numbers in the fall of 1998 when, as a U.S. Congresswoman, she was traveling on Falkland Road in Bombay, India, where one of the worst brothels in the world is located. She did know that she could not witness the "hopeless faces of desperate women and children forced into prostitution" and do nothing to help them. That's when she decided to form Shared Hope International (*www.sharedhope.org*) to give enslaved and trafficked women and children around the world a chance for a better life.

Shared Hope International is a nonprofit organization whose mission is "to rescue and restore women and children in crisis" and "to prevent and eradicate sex trafficking and slavery through education and public awareness." Shared Hope International uses a three-pronged strategy to help women and children:

1. *Prevent.* Their research and investigative work has led to the creation of the War Against Trafficking Alliance (which has held several world summits, gathering leaders from around the world), Predator Project (which has, among other things, conducted underground investigations in more than fourteen countries and increased prosecution laws in more than six countries), and Defenders USA (a campaign started on Father's Day 2006 specifically for men who want to help).

2. *Rescue.* Their interventions, outreach brochures, and HIV clinics have freed and treated women and children in countries from India to the Netherlands.

3. *Restore.* Their Homes of Hope are not only a place of refuge for rescued women and children, but they also provide health care, education, job training, and economic development programs so women can become financially free.

Since its formation, Shared Hope International has been a leader in the worldwide movement to eradicate sexual slavery. As the organization says on its Web site, "We will not give up. We will continue going into the darkness, rescuing and restoring young women and precious children—one life at a time." I look forward to the day when there is no longer a need for them to do so.

Here's an Idea You Can Do for the World *Today* . . . Check out *www.sharedhope.org* to learn more about sex trafficking and slavery and how you can help make a difference, locally, nationally, or internationally.

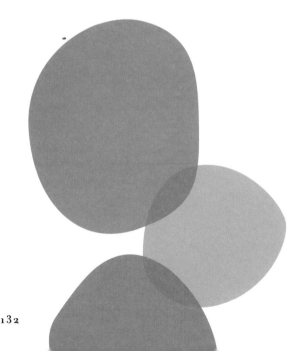

A *Doing for the World* Story

Many of us can look back on our lives and remember one or two moments that influenced us the most. For Meagan, one of those moments occurred when she was fourteen years old. She was watching the news with her family and was just plain angry about the one-sad-story-after-another that was being reported. That's when her dad said to her, "Meagan, there are enough people in this world who complain about things, but not enough people who do anything about them." In that moment, Meagan decided *she* was going to be one of those people who did something to make the world a better place.

As Meagan watched the Tiananmen Square massacre unfold while she was in high school and the Rwandan genocide occur the summer after she graduated, she decided she wanted to become an advocate for people, especially people who aren't able to stand up for themselves. Meagan will tell you that children are being sold into slavery and that the world has more slaves now than it did during the 400 years of the transatlantic slave trade. What's more, millions of people are dying from AIDS, and both the disease and the resulting deaths are preventable. Sitting by and doing nothing about the issues that matter to her is something Meagan cannot and will not ever do.

One of the ways Meagan has chosen to help others is through teaching. Not only has she worked as a teacher in the public and private sector in her home state of Georgia, she also spent a year studying and leading study groups in China, and she is currently teaching in Tanzania. Working with a ministry in Arusha (a city near Mount Kilimanjaro), Meagan is starting new schools in several villages, developing and training teachers already in schools, teaching at a Christian teachers training college, and helping with the child sponsorship programs. Because of the work Meagan is doing, some of the world's poorest children are able to eat vitamin-enriched porridge on a regular basis, enjoy a hug from a teacher who values them, and receive the kind of education that could help them break the cycle of poverty for good.

One of the schools Meagan has helped build is for orphans, many of whom are HIV positive. As Meagan says, all children deserve an education, no matter how long they are expected to live. In her life, Meagan has seen firsthand the sad-kind-of-stories that many of us only ever hear about on television. She has seen someone who was once vibrant and alive reduced to a skeleton as AIDS took its toll. She has seen (and smelled) the kind of filth and flies severe poverty brings. And she refuses to let any of her experiences overwhelm her into inaction. Wouldn't it be wonderful if each of us followed in her footsteps and said, "Here's what *I* am ready to do"?

Wouldn't the World Be a Better Place If . . .

Congresswoman Patricia Schroeder once said, "Our work as citizens is a lot like housework: It never ends. We can either wring our hands in despair or use them to roll up our shirtsleeves and try to find new ways to make a difference." One of the best things each of us can do for the world is roll up our sleeves and choose to make a difference. Think of it this way: housework may never stop, but if each of us chose to make a difference, perhaps our need to make a difference would stop being so pervasive.

The *Doing Whatever It Takes* Proclamation

Dear Present and Future Generations:

I want you to know that from this moment forward I am committed to doing whatever it takes to make the world a better place. Even if I

* ❄ Hear a story on the news that makes me cry

* ❄ Hear a story on the news that makes me want to throw the television out the window

* ❄ Worry that my actions aren't the right ones

* ❄ Worry that my actions aren't enough

* ❄ Never see any results from my actions

* ❄ Never hear any thanks for my actions

I will always choose to roll up my sleeves (or put on an old shirt) and look for new ways to make a difference (no matter how hard it will be or how dirty my shirt may get)!

Name _____ Date _____

A *Doing for the World* Story

For as long as she can remember, Pat has known that there are people in the world in need. When she was in first grade, her teacher often spoke to her class about children who didn't have food or clothes (much less toys to play with). Even though Pat grew up in a middle-class family, she understood that there were people around the world who had less than she did. She also always wanted to be able to help them.

It's probably no surprise that Pat studied economics and accounting, serving as a CPA, controller, and eventually a chief financial officer for several corporations throughout the 1980s and 1990s. Then, in 2000, Pat took a trip that changed her life (and eventually the lives of many people around the world). While staying in Chachapoyas, a remote region in the upper Amazon of Peru, Pat realized the villagers needed a way to make money that would improve their quality of life without destroying their unique culture in the process. Pat also realized she knew how she could make a difference.

Working with the villagers, Pat coordinated the building of a ceramics kiln and arranged for teachers to show the villagers how they could use nearby natural resources to create wares to sell to tourists and in the local markets. From this initial "Tools for Sustainability" project (which has led to great prosperity for the villagers, including a roof for the previously exposed and damp village school), Pat formed the International Fund for Economic Development (*www.IFED-US.org*), which became a nonprofit organization in 2002.

Pat and IFED have given people around the world tools for creating a sustainable income source. Pat has sent sewing machines to the Amazon library in Yanamono, Peru, to help the women develop sewing skills, enabling them to start a co-op to sell their wares. She has worked with CARE (a leading humanitarian organization fighting global poverty) and the Peace Corps to deliver donated computers to Ancash, a remote region of the Andes where the villagers speak an ancient dialect called "Quechua," so that villages with limited access to teachers could have a greater opportunity to educate their children. And she has helped educate Bengbu residents in the Chinese province of Anhui about the sanitation and health risks of pollution and litter so they wouldn't destroy the natural resources available to them.

For Pat, her goal in helping people around the world is *not* to become irreplaceable to them. Instead, Pat understands the importance of giving people tools so they can thrive on their own. She also understands that honoring people . . . and the diversity of their cultures . . . is just as important.

Wouldn't the World Be a Better Place If . . .

Marian Wright Edelman once said, "Education is for improving the lives of others and for leaving your community and the world better than you found it." Whether we travel five minutes or five countries from home, we can teach people ways to become independent, self-sufficient, and successful. We can also do so while loving people and cultures for who and what they are, instead of trying to change or destroy them.

A Brave, Beautiful, and Brilliant Possibility

I don't know about you, but when I think about all the amazing things that women have done for the world, it's hard to believe that we still live in a world that doesn't fully recognize how much women have to offer. In this day and age, it's mind-boggling that women are still earning less money than men and that we are still discussing whether a woman could be president of this country (though maybe by the time you're reading this that topic will no longer be in need of discussion or debate). It's mind-boggling that, in other parts of the world, women are denied education, health care, and the freedom to decide whose underwear they'll see crumpled by the shower in the morning.

I think it's time to say, "Enough already!" The world needs both men *and* women, and it is time for every person and every culture on this planet to see women as the equal, full-rights and full-pay-deserving contributors we are.

Here's an idea. Like our founding fathers did years ago, let's create a Declaration of Independence, only ours truly will be for *all* people, of *all* ages, in *all* countries.

Perhaps it could say something like:

We hold these truths to be completely obvious (and a long time in coming). That every woman on this planet deserves the freedom to:

❋ Live where she wants to live.

❋ Live how she wants to live.

❋ Live with whomever she wants to live with.

❋ Do what makes her happy.

❋ Not do what makes her unhappy.

❋ Decide what she does or does not do with her body.

❋ Never have to use her body for food or survival.

❋ Keep the money that she earns.

❋ Earn the same amount of money as her equally qualified male counterparts.

❋ Live in a world where she is always respected, valued, cherished, loved, and safe, and is never seen by anyone as an object, possession, or servant.

Imagine if women everywhere enjoyed these basic freedoms. Imagine if women everywhere really were free to say *Yes* to *their* choices instead of being forced to live someone else's. Imagine what kind of world we could and would create (and imagine how happy that world would be). Join me as a Declaration of Independence signatory, and let's create that kind of twenty-first-century world. Let's be the founding females for the estrogen-celebrating, women-rock world every woman deserves. Women everywhere, present and future, are counting on us. The great thing is, together, we have all the power we need to make a difference!

What brave, beautiful, and brilliant possibilities can YOU suggest?

A *Doing for the World* Story

Lucky and Bonnie first met in 1999, when they were the first two people to sign up for a workshop in Santa Barbara with author and futurist Barbara Marx Hubbard. At first glance, you couldn't find two people who were from more different backgrounds. Lucky had been actively involved in the women's movement since the 1970s, and she had never been shy about lacing up her marching boots or speaking out about causes and issues that mattered to her. Bonnie had been married three times to three very powerful men, and her life had been more focused on her husbands' careers than her ability to be her own person. But as Lucky and Bonnie soon learned, they share something quite important in common: a desire to figure out who they are and what matters most to them . . . and to help women everywhere do the same.

As Lucky and Bonnie got to know one another and became friends, they began to feel like there was a project they were meant to collaborate on. The idea for that project came to them on March 8, 2005, which happened to be International Women's Day. Lucky and Bonnie had been invited by Deborah Koppel Mitchell, the publisher of *Spheres Circle* magazine, to speak to a group of fifty women in Los Angeles who were each as remarkable and dynamic in their passion for women's rights as they were different and unique in the way they lived their lives. As Lucky and

Bonnie were driving back to Santa Barbara at the end of the day, they were talking about how wonderful it was to be among a group of women where everyone was valued for being exactly who they are . . . and who they want to become. That's when Lucky and Bonnie realized what they were meant to do together: they decided to create an organization called Evolutionary Women (*www.evolutionarywomen.org*) so they could help women everywhere evolve and grow, and live the kind of lives they most wanted to live.

Since Evolutionary Women was "born" (as Bonnie likes to describe it), Lucky and Bonnie have been busy doing exactly what they envisioned. They have led Evolutionary Women retreats in which women have explored who they are, what matters most to them, and what new possibilities they are ready to embrace. They have also helped many women, myself included, gain the courage needed to take those first or next steps into the unknown, be it toward a new life as a single woman, the boardroom as the head of a company, and the many other places that women are going.

Lucky and Bonnie deeply believe that *every* woman in the world has a contribution to make. They also believe that *every* contribution . . . of every size and on every level . . . is valuable (as they say, it can be "for your house or the White House"). They understand that part of making the world a better place is making the world a place where women everywhere can easily and confidently say, "This is who I am. This is what I want to do. And whatever that looks like is up to me, is wonderful, and is always enough." Because of Lucky and Bonnie, more women in the world are now able to do just that.

Wouldn't the World Be a Better Place If . . .

Janis Joplin once said, "Don't compromise yourself. You're all you've got." Choosing to live to your highest potential is one of the best gifts you can ever give to the world. Look at it this way: Every woman who chooses to live without compromising what matters most to her is an example to every woman who hasn't yet made (or isn't able to make) that choice. And as more women gain the courage (and the freedom) to live their lives on their own terms, we grow closer to creating a world where *every* woman can enjoy the kind of future that she wants.

An Awesome Idea in Action

Creating a world where every woman is free to express her highest potential in the way that means the most to her (as Bonnie and Lucky desire) is an amazing vision to have. An important step we must take to create that world is to help women gain an equal voice in governments and governing bodies around the world. The Women's Environment and Development Organization (WEDO; *www.wedo.org*) has been working to achieve that very goal since it was founded in 1991 by former U.S. Congresswoman Bella Abzug (who was born just one month before women in the United States earned the right to vote) and feminist activist and journalist Mim Kelber.

WEDO is an international organization that gathers women from around the world to share experiences and expertise, and to take action in the United Nations and other international policymaking arenas. Since its founding, WEDO has helped women gain a voice in many important international conferences. One example occurred just prior to the United Nations Conference on Environment and Development (UNCED) in 1992. WEDO gathered more than 1,500 women from eighty-three countries for the World Women's Congress for a Healthy Planet, which resulted in the Women's Action Agenda 21 (an outline "for a healthy and peaceful planet that was the basis for introducing gender equality in the official UNCED final documents").

WEDO has also organized the Women's Caucus at a variety of United Nations conferences, including the UN International Conference on Population and Development in Egypt in 1994 and the UN World Conference on Human Settlements (HABITAT) in Turkey in 1996.

Today, WEDO focuses on creating women's equality around the world in four areas:

1. *Gender and governance*, which seeks "women's full and equal access to all areas and all levels of public life." (Check out their "Global 50/50 Campaign to Get the Balance Right!" in national parliaments and cabinets.)

2. *Sustainable development*, which fosters "development that is ecologically sound, economically viable, and socially just, and works to strengthen the alliances between the women's and environmental movements."

3. *Economic and social justice*, which focuses on "poverty eradication, international trade, debt cancellation, and resource allocation." (Check out their "MisFortune 500" project that exposes corporations that "violate women's rights, threaten lives and livelihoods, and destroy the environment.")

4. *U.S. global policy*, which analyzes U.S. foreign policy and works to build alliances with U.S. groups to

counter any negative impacts U.S. policy may have "on women living in the U.S. and around the world."

WEDO was created to bring women together and give us a voice in a greater and equal scale around the world. As their Web site says, it's all about "a healthy and peaceful planet, economic and social justice, and human rights for all." Why would anyone want to argue with that?

Here's an Idea You Can Do for the World *Today* . . . Check out *www.wedo.org* to learn more about all the ways WEDO is working to give every woman in every country an equal voice and equal chance to live to her highest, best, and most prosperous potential.

A *Doing for the World* Story

Tamara has always been someone who values and appreciates people from all walks of life. As a child, she watched her father help drug addicts, young women who were pregnant and had no place to go, and local prisoners (in fact, her family would often pick up a prisoner and take him to church on Sundays). As an adult, she has both traveled and lived overseas (her time in Brussels was a particular favorite). Learning about other people and other cultures is something Tamara loves the most.

A few years ago, when Tamara was finishing her master's in theology, a professor recommended that she spend a year studying in Israel. Tamara had, as she calls it, a "keen sense" that her understanding of peaceful solutions would grow during her trip, and she began classes at Jerusalem University College just after her arrival in the region in late August 2001. Her Modern Middle East Politics class quickly became one of her favorites, and on the morning of September 11 (hours before morning dawned in the United States), her professor lectured on the fragility of peace in the Middle East. Tamara and a friend stayed after class that morning to discuss the subject even further with their professor, and Tamara remembers leaving an hour later humming the R.E.M. song, "It's the End of the World as We Know It." Just a few hours later, she watched in horror from a computer lab as the Twin Towers fell in New York.

Tamara chose to remain in the Middle East for the next ten months as she had planned, eventually moving and switching schools when her college was closed due to escalating violence. Despite the violence nearby and the violence at home, Tamara's desire to study peace and peaceful solutions deepened. She volunteered with Rabbis for Human Rights (a local organization promoting justice and equity for Jews, Palestinians, and Bedouins), shared conversations and cake with the Greek archbishop and coffee with the Syrian Mukhtar (the head of Jerusalem's Syrian Orthodox community), and enjoyed spending time with Jews, Muslims, Palestinians, Christians, Domari Gypsies, and anyone else she met. She also experienced amazing hospitality . . . from *everyone*! (You can read more about Tamara's travels in the Middle East in her book *Sacred Encounters from Rome to Jerusalem*.)

Of all the things Tamara said about her time in the Middle East, one of my favorites is this: "Everyone has a longing to interact. We are so much more human when we engage others than when we isolate." And of all the observations she can share with the world, I think one of the greatest is, "When we interact with other cultures and people who are different than us, we can realize that there is something to learn rather than something to fear." As Tamara calls it, we can have "interactions of grace" with everyone we meet. We can be willing to share a meal or a laugh rather than build a wall (or fire a gun). We can choose to see every person on the planet as a person of significance. And we can decide to act (and vote) accordingly.

Wouldn't the World Be a Better Place If . . .

Maya Angelou said, "We should all know that diversity makes for a rich tapestry, and we must understand that all the threads of the tapestry are equal in value no matter what their color." At the end of the day, believing this brave, beautiful, and brilliant quote . . . and acting accordingly . . . is perhaps the best gift we can ever give to each other and to the world.

What Do YOU Want to Do for the World?

Pearl Buck once said, "All things are possible until they are proved impossible —even the impossible may only be so, as of now." Are you ready, willing, and able to see what's possible? And are you ready, willing, and able to act accordingly?

Are you ready to help the world's children speak up and speak out (especially when few people are listening)? Are you ready to help women and communities become self-sufficient in the ways that make the most sense for them?

Are you willing to reduce, reuse, or recycle (even if the people around you aren't)? Are you willing to share a meal with everyone (no matter where they are from)? Are you willing to live without compromise (and help others do the same) especially when big changes may result?

Are you able to see the world as a safe and friendly place (despite the latest tragedy that seems to say otherwise)? And, are you able to choose to make a difference (even when you are angry, upset, or tempted to complain about things instead)?

If you ran the world, and were the person everyone looked upon to make the world a better place, could you teach people the lesson that so many of the women in this book have learned: that we really are more alike than different? Could you help people see past the past and imagine a better way for tomorrow? Could you help people realize that we can choose to not punish an entire country (or not see an entire culture as our enemy) because of the actions that certain individuals take? Could you help people see that what is past their borders and boundaries is not something they need to fear (or arm themselves against or protect themselves from)?

Helen Keller once said, "I am only one, but still I am one. I cannot do everything, but still I can do something; and because I cannot do everything, I will not refuse to do something that I can do."

Right now, YOU really can help someone or some cause somewhere. YOU really can do something to make the world a better place. If each of us were ready, willing, and able to help in just one of the ways that we want to help . . . in the way that means the most to us . . . we would make the kind of beautiful difference and create the kind of beautiful future everyone deserves! Like Helen Keller said, you do not have to do everything, just the something that you can do. **What is the "something" that YOU are ready, willing, and able to do for the world?**

The Brave, Beautiful, and Brilliant Things
I Want to Do for the World

_____

_____

_____

_____

_____

_____

_____

_____

_____

Epilogue

Eleanor Roosevelt shared one of the best thoughts ever when she said, "The future belongs to those who believe in the beauty of their dreams." Whatever future you dream of . . . be it for yourself, your loved ones, your community, or the world . . . know that you have the power to believe that such a future is possible. You also have the power to create that future today (and no fun scepter or shiny crown on your head is required to start).

You don't actually need to be in charge of the world to change the world (or to change things for yourself, your loved ones, or your community). You just need to be ready, willing, and able to act . . . even and especially when you are having doubts, when you think the well-intentioned but ultimately clueless set are right to question your sanity, or when your heart gets broken along the way. You need to be ready, willing, and able to trust your instincts . . . and to get started even if you don't have everything figured out.

When I think about all the women whose stories appear in this book . . . when I think about *all* the brave, beautiful, and brilliant things they have done, are doing, or want to do . . . there's something even more amazing then all their stories individually or combined: the fact that there are billions of women in the world with billions of brave, beautiful, and brilliant ideas for making the world a better place. It is my hope that this book helps women everywhere realize that they are just as powerful, able, and capable as every woman I have written about. It is my hope that this book inspires these women to put their awesome ideas into immediate action. And it is my hope that someday soon we will be living in a world where women everywhere are free to do just that. What an amazing day . . . and dare I say a better world . . . that would certainly be!

I wish you all the best with whatever it is YOU are ready, willing, and able to do to make the world a better place. I'm excited to see the cumulative efforts from all of us!

Shelly Rachanow

Share Your Brave, Beautiful, and Brilliant Ideas

Do you have a brave, beautiful, and brilliant idea that YOU are ready to do (or are already doing) for yourself, your loved ones, your community, or the world? Log onto *www.What-WouldYouDoIfYouRanTheWorld.com* and share your ideas with women everywhere. One of the most beautiful things about women is the way we encourage and inspire each other. Just imagine who your ideas may touch . . . and what great things could happen in the world as a result . . . if you log on today!

Acknowledgments

I am so grateful to the many fabulous people who helped make this book possible:

To the entire staff of Red Wheel · Weiser · Conari: Thank you for publishing books that make a difference in people's lives and for making my publishing dream come true. Special thanks to *Jan Johnson, Michael Kerber, Brenda Knight, Bonni Hamilton,* and *Rachel Leach.*

To Karyn, Liz, Mindy, Marlene, Adrienne, Jen, Emily, Elisabeth, Rebecca, Jan, Erica, Mom, Nadeen, Robin, Aly, Shannon, Judee, Leslie, Patty, Jyn, Andrea, Mary, Meagan, Pat, Lucky, Bonnie, and Tamara: Thank you for sharing your stories with me and for being the amazing women you are. You inspire me!

To Karyn Allen, Robin Alva, Alene Kramer, Hilary Mann, Rebecca McLaren, and Jessica McKinney: Thank you for reading this book as I was writing it and for all the wonderful feedback you provided.

To my mom, Sally; my father, Jerry; my sister, Mindy; my brother, Gary; my brother-in-law, Don; and my nephew, Dylan: Thank you for all the extra love and support you gave me through the writing of this book.

To Dr. Heather Dawn Clark: Thank you for being my friend and mentor, and for your reminder about the importance of joy when I most needed one.

And to my dear friends Elisabeth Andre, Peggy Chippeaux, Jyn Hall, Mark Lacey, Hilary Mann, Jon McDonald, and Jon Williams: Thank you for being the kind of friends who are always there for me and who love me no matter what. My life is happier because I know you.

About the Author

Shelly Rachanow comes from a long line of butt-kicking women. She is a graduate of George Washington University and Emory University School of Law. Shelly Rachanow is also the author of *If Women Ran the World Sh*t Would Get Done*. She lives in San Clemente, California.

To Our Readers

Conari Press, an imprint of Red Wheel/Weiser, publishes books on topics ranging from spirituality, personal growth, and relationships to women's issues, parenting, and social issues. Our mission is to publish quality books that will make a difference in people's lives — how we feel about ourselves and how we relate to one another. We value integrity, compassion, and receptivity, both in the books we publish and in the way we do business.

Our readers are our most important resource, and we value your input, suggestions, and ideas about what you would like to see published. Please feel free to contact us, to request our latest book catalog, or to be added to our mailing list.

Conari Press
An imprint of Red Wheel/Weiser, LLC
500 Third Sreet, Suite 230
San Francisco, CA 94107
www.redwheelweiser.com